LOVING GOD WITH
ALL YOUR MIND

LOVING GOD WITH ALL YOUR MIND

How to Survive and Prosper
As a Christian in the Secular University
and Post-Christian Culture

Gene Edward Veith, Jr.

CROSSWAY BOOKS • WESTCHESTER, ILLINOIS
A DIVISION OF GOOD NEWS PUBLISHERS

Cover Photo: WOODMANSTERNE, Howard Moore (England). Trinity College Library, Cambridge

Book Design: K. L. Mulder

First printing, 1987

Printed in the United States of America

Library of Congress Catalog Card Number 87-70460

ISBN 0-89107-435-X

All Scripture quotations, unless otherwise indicated, are taken from the *Revised Standard Version* of the Bible, copyright © 1946, 1952, 1971, 1973.

For Paul, Joanna, and Mary

TABLE OF

CONTENTS

1 Introduction   9

Part I Learning As a Christian Vocation
2 Education and the Bible   15
3 Daniel at the University of Babylon   25

Part II The Modern Mind
4 The Attacks Against Christianity   39
5 The Exclusion of God   53
6 Traditionalists and Progressives   63
7 The Moral Issues   73
8 Intellectual Combat   85

Part III The Christian Mind
9   The Communion of the Saints   91
10 The Magicians and the Enchanters   107
11 Creation and Creativity   119
12 Christianity As an Intellectual Framework   131
13 Conclusion: Loving God with All Your Mind   143

Notes   151

ONE

INTRODUCTION

*C*hristians should use and develop their minds. The mental faculties of the human mind—the power to think, to discover, to wonder, and to imagine—are precious gifts of God. The Christian who pursues knowledge, seeks education, and explores even the most "secular" subjects is fulfilling a Christian vocation that is pleasing to God and of great importance to the Church. The Bible, by precept and example, affirms this and opens up the whole realm of human knowledge to the Christian. This is my main thesis.

When Christians do pursue the whole realm of human knowledge, however, they often run into some obstacles. This is especially so today. Christian assumptions are not generally recognized in academia or in our culture in general. Christians often find their faith challenged when they become involved in the arts, the sciences, the social sciences, and other professions. Christianity is clearly not in vogue with the "intellectual establishment."

When Christians realize that there are some basic discrepancies between their faith and modern thought, they often do one of two things: They withdraw or they compromise. Evangelical students who go to a secular university are often shocked and disoriented when they discover that their professors, textbooks, and classmates do not share their faith. Some of them, not knowing how to deal with the difficult issues they are facing, quit school. Others, tragically, abandon their faith. Overwhelmed by the power and prestige of secularist academia, and being unable to draw on the intellectual resources of the Christian faith, they drift away from Christ.

Another common option is to compromise, to reinterpret Christian doctrine according to modern ways of thinking. This is the route to theological liberalism. It is possible to become so enraptured by one's academic discipline that its answers to problems start to seem more authoritative than the Bible's. Those who crave academic respectability and acceptance by peers and colleagues may not be willing to abandon Christianity entirely; instead, they often reinterpret it according to contemporary fashions and values. In doing so, the hard-edged faith that has always been a scandal and a stumbling-block to the world is changed into something less.

This book argues that it is possible for Christians to engage the modern intellectual world without weakening or compromising their faith. Christians in fact need to do so, both for the sake of the Church and for the sake of a world that is starving for the truth of the gospel.

Christians need to be aware, though, of the contours of modern thought. They need to know what to expect and how to deal with some of the challenges to the Christian faith that they will encounter. They also need to know the positive side, how Christian truth genuinely opens up the mind, providing a framework that embraces all knowledge and that gives a basis for curiosity, creativity, and all the energy of learning for the glory of God.

What I have to say will apply to the whole climate of modern thought as it appears almost everywhere in our culture, but my focus will be on the secular university. This is where that thought is engendered and nourished, and it is the point of encounter for most Christians. Although this book is intended mainly as an exposition and application of Scripture, it also draws on my own experiences. As an undergraduate I made many of the mistakes that I will be counseling others to avoid. When I was a graduate student, drawing on the power of the Bible and the support of fellow-Christians, I began to see the strength of the Christian perspective in modern academia. Today I am a professor. Having taught English in both secular and Christian colleges and having become a small part of the "intellectual establishment" in my own research and dealing with colleagues and students, I make bold here to offer an insider's view of academia and the modern intellectual world.

This book is divided into three parts. The first section presents the Biblical case for "secular learning." It argues that the life of the mind—the process of learning and pursuing knowledge of every kind—is a legitimate, God-pleasing calling for a Christian. It focuses upon the particular example of Daniel as a Biblical model of a believer pursuing knowledge in an unbelieving world.

The second section provides an overview of the modern mind, describing the assumptions and characteristics of the current intellectual establishment as seen especially in the modern academic climate. That section will examine the various attacks and temptations that Christians will face from that quarter, but it will not be totally negative. Christians can contribute to modern thought in some important ways and can flourish even in an environment that seems hostile.

The third section describes "the Christian mind." In it I argue that Christianity provides an intellectual framework that is actually superior to any other world view for the pursuit of knowledge. Looking at history and at the current intellectual roadblocks that secularist thinkers are experiencing, I suggest that only Christianity can account for the complexity and the open-endedness required for true learning. Christianity gives a conceptual foundation for creativity, comprehensiveness, and mystery, so that the pursuit of all truth can be energized by the love of God.

The new student trying to understand and cope with university life, the scholar seriously trying to reconcile the demands of an academic career with the demands of the Christian faith, Christian teachers in public schools, pastors trying to minister to a modern congregation, Christian psychologists, journalists, scientists, artists—nearly all Christians today will face the conflicts and the possibilities that I will be describing. I offer here a map of the modern intellectual world that might prove helpful to a Christian trying to navigate its sometimes troubled waters. I also wish to show that

Christians do not need to be afraid to think, that Christians
in fact have advantages over non-Christians when it comes to
using their minds. God is the source of all truth, and every
discovery is a means of glorifying Him. Just as Jesus Christ
commands us to love the Lord our God with all of our heart,
our soul, and our strength, He also commands us to love Him
with all of our mind (Mark 12:30). This book tries to explore
what that can mean and what it can lead to.

PART ONE

LEARNING AS A CHRISTIAN VOCATION

T W O

EDUCATION AND
THE BIBLE

*S*hould a Christian get involved in the world's intellectual discoveries and intellectual battles? Does the university have anything to teach a Christian, or is it simply another pagan mission field? How does "secular learning" fit in with the knowledge of God? Christians trying to decide whether or not to go to college (or to stay in college) often ask these questions. Christians in other professions ask similar questions: Should Christians read books by non-Christians? Can a Christian learn from non-Christian psychologists, scientists, or artists? All believers must walk the tightrope of being in the world but not of the world and must continually deal with such questions. To find answers, one should begin by asking God—that is, by studying the Scriptures.

SECULAR EDUCATION IN THE BIBLE

The Bible gives many examples of people who were both highly educated in the knowledge of the day and who were also heroes of the faith. Moses was "instructed in all the wisdom of the Egyptians" (Acts 7:22), which would have been considerable. Daniel, Shadrach, Meshach, and Abednego were at the court of Nebuchadnezzar—den of lions, fiery furnace, and all—precisely so they could learn the knowledge of the Chaldeans (Daniel 1).

Paul studied "at the feet of Gamaliel" (Acts 22:3), who conducted the most distinguished academy of first-century Judaism. Paul's hometown, Tarsus, was famous for its university. We do not know if he was influenced directly by the great Hellenic academy at Tarsus, but from his mastery of Greek, including his citations of Greek drama and his occasional employment of classical rhetoric, it is apparent that Paul was well-acquainted with Greek and Roman thought. Paul's sophisticated education was recognized by Festus, who worried that "your great learning is turning you mad" (Acts 26:24), a very real occupational hazard.

Although Festus remained unconvinced, another Roman official, Sergius Paulus, became Paul's first convert mentioned in Scripture. Praised as a "man of intelligence" (Acts 13:7), this proconsul of Cyprus must have been highly educated. The same office was held at Cilicia by Cicero, one of the greatest minds of Rome.[1]

Paul's great coworker Apollos was from the Egyptian city of Alexandria, the premier center of Greco-Roman thought.[2] The library of Alexandria was one of the wonders of the world, and its "museum" was, in effect, the major university of the age. Described in the Bible as both an Alexandrian and as "an eloquent man" (Acts 18:24), Apollos must have been trained in the rhetoric and dialectic for which Alexandria was famous. Judging by his Greek name, Apollos must have been a Hellenized Jew, a follower of the Old Testament who was also open to the classical culture around him. Apollos was not only learned, but he was also "mighty in the Scriptures" (Acts 18:24, KJV). He placed his analytical and intellectual powers at the service of Christ's Kingdom:

> When he arrived, he greatly helped those who through grace had believed, for he powerfully confuted the Jews in public, showing by the scriptures that the Christ was Jesus. (Acts 18:27, 28)

Having earthly knowledge is, of course, no substitute for the work of the gospel. "Not many of you were wise according to worldly standards," observes Paul (1 Corinthians 1:26), thereby indicating that a few of them were. It must not be forgotten that "the world did not know God through wisdom" (1 Corinthians 1:21). Solomon's great wisdom, for example, did not prevent him from falling away into idolatry.

Still, the Bible leaves no doubt that Solomon's wide-ranging knowledge was a gift and a blessing from God:

> And God gave Solomon wisdom and understanding beyond measure, and largeness of mind like the sand on the seashore, so that Solomon's wisdom surpassed all the wisdom of all the people of the east, and all the wisdom of Egypt. For he was wiser than all other men, wiser than Ethan the Ezrahite, and Heman, Calcol, and Darda, the sons of Mahol; and his fame was in all the nations round about. He also uttered three thousand proverbs; and his songs were a thousand and five. He spoke of trees, from the cedar that is in Lebanon to the hyssop that grows out of the wall; he spoke also of beasts, and of birds, and of reptiles, and of fish. And men came from all peoples to hear the wisdom of Solomon, and from all the kings of the earth, who had heard of his wisdom. (1 Kings 4:29-34)

Solomon's famous wisdom was not only moral discernment. Solomon is described here as a philosopher, a poet, a musician, and a natural scientist. "He spoke of trees . . . of beasts, and of birds, and of reptiles, and of fish." In other words, according to the Bible, Solomon was a biologist. Nearly every type of knowledge, from the arts to biological science, from music to psychology, was poured out upon Solomon by the Creator of them all. For God is always portrayed as the source of all true knowledge, and intellectual ability is His gift.

EDUCATION AND THE BIBLE

There is another sense in which Scripture by its very nature upholds education. God chose to reveal Himself by means of a book. He communicates to us not primarily by visions, mystical experiences, or inner voices, but by His Word. Christians believe that we meet God and enter into a direct, personal contact with Him when we sit down and read a book, the Holy Bible. Therefore, reading is for Christians literally a sacred gift and obligation.

The ability to read is now taken for granted. Historically, however, this has not been the case. The ability to read is not common in world cultures. In the relatively few civilizations that developed writing, only the elite could read and thereby wield the power that reading made possible. Literacy, however, has always been nourished by the Church.

In fact, the high rate of literacy in our culture and the very existence of modern educational institutions are due to the centrality of the Bible in the Christian faith. In ancient times, when many of the surrounding tribes did not even have an alphabet, and when those that did restricted their use to the bureaucrats, the businessmen, and the priests who sought to protect their mysteries from the masses, every Hebrew boy was learning how to read God's Word.

During the Middle Ages, books had to be copied out by hand, making them very rare and expensive. Most people, including the very wealthy, could not read anyway. Yet the Church could not exist without the Bible. Copies of the Scriptures were laboriously and lovingly inscribed by hand. The great universities of Europe, such as Oxford and the Sorbonne, were founded to train the ministers of the Church in Scripture. (The historic American universities—Harvard, Princeton, and the majority of all private colleges—were founded for the same purpose much later.) Ministers at least must be able to read and to understand Christian doctrine in order to fulfill their function as teachers of God's Word. In fact, the term *clergy* and its related form *clerk* often simply referred to someone who could read. (As late as the nineteenth century, a criminal could escape hanging by claiming "benefit of clergy," which he did by proving that he could read, a skill that was too valuable to lose to the hangman.)[3]

That the medieval Church to a certain extent fell into superstition and error, neglecting the authority of Scripture in favor of human traditions, was probably due in large measure to the literal scarcity of Bibles and of people who could read them. Even many of the clergy had become shamefully uneducated. Many churches did not even own a Bible. Since they had to be copied out by hand, they were enormously expensive. With the printing press, however, books could be mass-produced and universal literacy became possible. With this new technology, everyone could have access to a Bible and could have personal contact with the Word of God. Luther's greatest work as a Reformer was his translation of the Bible into the language of the people. Another legacy of Luther, which makes him a major figure for all of our culture and not only the Church, was the development of universal education. All classes of people were to be taught how to read so they could know for themselves the fullness of God's will and His love as communicated in the Scriptures.

Even today, literacy training is part of the work of evangelism. Missionaries such as the Wycliffe translators typically go into an area to learn the language of the people, translate the Bible into their language, and then teach them how to read it. The Word of God is what subsequently brings them to faith in Christ. Once the people of these primitive tribes learn how to read, though, other worlds open up to them. Their ability to read the Bible also gives them access to other kinds of knowledge, to modern technology and health care, to the possibility of escaping from poverty and social repression. Their ability to read the Bible opens up the whole scope of knowledge.

THE BIBLE AND OTHER KINDS OF KNOWLEDGE

If a person believes that the Bible is the authoritative and holy Word of God, supremely worthy of study and understanding, other kinds of knowledge in addition to the ability to read become very important. The languages chosen by God for His revelation are Hebrew and Greek. The knowledge of these ancient languages is thus a matter for more advanced study for those who wish to study God's Word exactly as He inspired it. Linguistics, the study of language in general, becomes essential in translating and rendering the Bible's message into modern languages. The Wycliffe missionaries are trained in the most rigorous methodology of modern scientific linguistics in order to carry out their work of trans-lation and evangelism.

Moreover, to understand fully the ancient Hebrew terms and references, a knowledge of history is indispensable. Geography, archaeology, and anthropology are all involved in a full understanding of the events of Scripture. The Bible also proclaims theological truths, which involve the vocabu-lary of philosophy and abstract discourse. The point is, even if a person desires to know only the Bible, that knowledge would have to involve a multitude of sophisticated academic disciplines.

Consider, for example, the Reformation. Martin Luther was a doctor of theology, a professor of the prestigious Uni-versity of Wittenberg. His discovery of the gospel, the good news of free forgiveness through Jesus Christ, came in the course of his academic preparation for a series of lectures on Romans. His translation of the Bible would have been impos-sible without his academic training and his intellectual and creative gifts. It depended further on the textual scholar-ship—a dry, painstaking, but fascinating academic disci-pline—of Erasmus, who prepared an authoritative edition of the Greek New Testament. Before, the New Testament had only been available in a Latin translation. Knowledge of the original Greek language depended, in turn, on the work of the Renaissance "humanists" who helped to recover the clas-sical languages. Luther was in touch with this new scholar-ship and was a master of Greek, as well as his own German language. He also depended upon his colleague Melanchthon, the notable Hebrew scholar and theologian.

The Reformation also depended upon the scientific and technological discoveries of the Renaissance. Were it not for the technological innovations that gave rise to the printing press—the developments in metallurgy and engineering, the countless interconnected discoveries that led to the mass pro-duction of books—the vernacular Bible would still never have reached the people who were starving for the Word of God.

There is an even deeper sense in which the Bible sup-ports the pursuit of knowledge. Historically, it was the Bible that swept away the superstitions of paganism and opened the door to modern science, technology, and culture.

THE BIBLE AND WESTERN THOUGHT

Modern Western thought has deep roots in Christianity and in a Biblical world view.[4] Even if contemporary scientists reject Christianity, they cannot escape its influence in the very way they think. For example, those of us in the West assume that time travels in a straight line. Physicists speculate about the beginning of the universe, biologists argue about how species change and develop, sociologists chart the progress of societies, and futurists of all kinds worry about the end of the human race. The assumption is that time has a beginning and an end. This linear view of time and human history comes from the Bible, which teaches that time has a beginning, the creation as described in Genesis 1, and that it rushes forward to its end, the Last Judgment as described in Revelation.

The ancient pagan civilizations, on the other hand, assumed that time is a series of cycles. The seasons and generations endlessly repeat one another. The cycles of day and night, summer and winter, birth and death continue forever, with no beginning and no end. There was no creation from nothing. The Babylonian creation myths describe how a god initiates a new phase of being, forming a world from a world that already exists. Pagan societies are relatively static. Progress, change, development are very difficult concepts for pagan cultures to understand.

Even those who oppose the Bible today nevertheless assume a Biblical model of time. Marxists may see religion as the "opiate of the people" and insist on a militant atheism, but they think in terms of change and apocalypse, with history moving to a last judgment when all oppressive social systems will wither away into a worker's paradise. Evolutionists also assume a linear model of time which derives from the Bible. The ancient Babylonians or Canaanites would scarcely be able to raise the question of the "origin of species." Nor would they be able to imagine a future very different from the past. Secular humanists of every type may ridicule the

Bible, but they cannot escape it; and in their obsession with change, calls for reform, doomsday warnings, and utopian visions, they continue to steal from it.

Another important example of Biblical assumptions in modern Western thought is the view of nature. Modern science could not have arisen without the Bible. For the Babylonians and Canaanites, nature was sacred. It was part of the gods. Nature was to be worshiped. It was to be treated with awe. It was to receive prayers. The ancient pagans were not romantics. They did not "appreciate nature." They were terrified of it. They offered blood sacrifices in the hopes of getting a better crop. They worried that if they violated a ritual taboo, the rains might not come or they might not be able to bear children. The gods and the natural forces they represent were to be placated, not loved. They might sometimes be magically manipulated, but never understood.

In contrast, the Bible insists that God is distinct from His creation. The pagan nature religions, which were often a temptation to the Hebrews as to us, were always opposed by the prophets and the other authors of Scripture. Nature was no longer to be seen as sacred. The "ghosts" which made nature a matter for fear and taboo were banished. As a result, nature could be seen in a different way. As the creation of a God who declared it "very good" (Genesis 1), nature was dependable and valuable. It could be studied. There were no tree-gods to offend—one could examine the tree in its physical createdness. Science became possible. Human beings no longer had to serve nature. Nature could serve human beings. Technology became possible. Modern science and technology, in their very origins, grew out of a Biblical world view.

Modern Western thought has its origins in our culture's Judeo-Christian heritage. Moreover, the very "secular" quality of much modern knowledge is part of that Biblical heritage. For the Hebrews, knowledge tainted by the pagan religions of their neighbors was always a problem. If that knowledge could be secularized—that is, divorced from the idolatrous world views that often accompanied it—then it could find its place within God's creation. That is still the problem for Christians today, to sort out truth from the false religious teachings in which it often is packaged. The problems come when secular fields cease being secular and presume to offer religious and moral judgments. Pure secular knowledge, unmixed with religious falsehood, presents few problems.

The centrality of the Bible for evangelical Christians means that they ought never to despise learning. By precept, by example, by its history, and by its very nature, the Bible opens up to us the whole world of truth. However, the pursuit of that truth in a sinful, nonbelieving world is not without its problems. The possibilities and the dangers of such an enterprise can perhaps best be illustrated by studying in detail a specific case history from the Bible: the education of Daniel.

THREE

DANIEL AT THE UNIVERSITY OF BABYLON

*M*ost people know about Daniel in the lions' den and Shadrach, Meshach, and Abednego in the fiery furnace. Many, though, perhaps do not realize what these young Hebrews were doing at the court of Nebuchadnezzar in the first place. They were there to study at the royal academy of Babylon. They were, in effect, college students.[1]

The experience of Daniel is, in many respects, remarkably parallel to the experience of Christians today. Christian students in a secular university or Christians facing modern culture and the modern intellectual world will often feel themselves to be exiles in a strange and hostile land, just as Daniel was. And yet the first chapter of Daniel suggests that it is possible for a believer in the true God to profit from the knowledge of the day. It points out the trials, temptations, and pressures that may be faced, but it also suggests how to deal with them. Daniel was able to learn the knowledge of the Babylonians without compromising the least doctrinal or moral point. In fact, Daniel, Shadrach, Meshach, and Abednego were able to thrive at the University of Babylon, their faith actually enabling them to outdo their pagan counterparts on their own terms. In trying to find a Biblical perspective on the value and hazards of the modern intellectual world, it will be helpful to study the example of Daniel in detail.

The first two verses of the book of Daniel record how the Babylonian king waged war against Jerusalem, took its leading citizens and the anointed king himself into captivity, and desecrated the holy temple, blasphemously offering the holy vessels of the sanctuary to the service of the false god Marduk (Daniel 1:1, 2). Nebuchadnezzar was oppressive, ruthless, and cruel. Babylon was in such enmity with God that it became a type and a foreshadowing of the reign of Antichrist (Revelation 18). Yet, "the king commanded Ashpenaz, his chief eunuch, to bring some of the people of Israel, both of the royal family and of the nobility, youths without blemish, handsome and skillful in all wisdom, endowed with knowledge, understanding learning, and competent to serve in the kings's palace, and to teach them the letters and language of the Chaldeans" (Daniel 1:3-7).

ACADEMIC PREREQUISITES

Nebuchadnezzar chose only people with specific academic gifts. Although he wanted students to be "handsome" and from the upper class (tacit requirements at some colleges even today), the rest of his list sums up, in remarkable detail and comprehensiveness, the prerequisites for receiving a successful education:

One must be "skillful in all wisdom"—that is, have the academic skills and techniques that are necessary for advanced learning. Becoming educated means mastering processes as well as accumulating knowledge. Skills such as reading, writing, managing, teaching, and problem-solving involve highly specific mental gymnastics that education depends on and develops.

One must be "endowed with knowledge"—that is, already have a fund of knowledge that may be built upon with further studies. Knowledge, if it is preserved and handed down, can accumulate. Many modern artists, philosophers, and theologians reject the knowledge of the past. Thus, they must continually start over again from ground zero, their vision restricted to their own narrow perspectives, making themselves artificially primitive. Modern technology, on the other hand, is relatively conservative in its acceptance of past discoveries, all of which can then build on each other to result in such collaborations as automobiles, televisions, and computers. Education conveys knowledge, but it also assumes knowledge.

One must "understand learning"—that is, be able to assimilate intellectually the material that is presented. Understanding is the faculty of synthesis, of pulling together the facts that have been learned and the skills that have been mastered, relating them to each other and discerning their implications. A person may know a host of facts and amaze everyone with a mastery of skill, but without understanding, without being able to use and to assimilate what has been learned, that person is scarcely educated.

Finally, one must be "competent to serve"—that is, have the necessary motivation and social skills to use what one has learned in service to other people. Becoming educated is not simply a matter of self-fulfillment, but its ultimate purpose, the Scripture reminds us, is service. The king was looking specifically for people who were "competent to serve in the king's palace," people with leadership abilities that could fit them for influential roles in government and the culture as a whole. Education opens up important and influential spheres of service—healing the sick, feeding the hungry, repairing families, rebuilding morality, reforming society—which call out for Christian involvement.

Such qualities as skill, knowledge, understanding, and service are not universal, but there were some Israelites with these gifts, just as today there are Christians with academic potential. Nebuchadnezzar gave these four Hebrews full economic support—sort of a full-ride scholarship—and commanded that "they were to be educated for three years, and at the end of that time they were to stand before the king" (1:15).

THE KING'S TABLE

It seems clear from the Bible that this three-year educational program was within the will of God. Daniel, Shadrach, Meshach, and Abednego had their academic talents from God, and it was His plan to bring them to this place of learning and influence. There can thus be nothing intrinsically wrong with their learning "the letters and language of the Chaldeans." We often think of modern universities as being non-Christian, but they would be bastions of fundamentalism compared to Babylon. As we have seen and will see further, modern Western thought has its origins in a Biblical world view, despite its current departures. Daniel, though, could hardly have read a cuneiform tablet without some reference to pagan deities and mythology. The Babylonians were masters of mathematics, astronomy, engineering, and administration, but their very real discoveries in these fields were thoroughly mythologized in the way they were understood. If Scripture indicates that Babylonian "letters and language" were nevertheless worthy of study, there should be nothing objectionable to a Christian about studying any legitimate field of contemporary thought, which, for all of its problems, is probably less shot-through with error than that of the Chaldeans.

There were certainly problems, however, for God's children in such an environment. No sooner had the four Hebrews arrived at court than they encountered a problem that seemed to jeopardize the whole venture. It is interesting that the conflict Scripture records is not over great world-view issues—not a debate over the merits of the Babylonian creation myth versus the account in Genesis—nor on important moral issues, such as the four having to reject the principle of cult prostitution as a means of worship. Rather, the issue was one that must have seemed to both sides so technical, so minor, so hard to explain.

> But Daniel resolved that he would not defile himself
> with the king's rich food, or with the wine which he
> drank; therefore he asked the chief of the eunuchs
> to allow him not to defile himself. (1:8)

The king was honoring the young men with food from his own table, lavish, exquisite food for these poverty-stricken exiles, a generous, even kind-hearted gesture on the part of Nebuchadnezzar. Yet, that food would not have been in accordance with the Mosaic dietary laws. Not only could the Hebrews not eat certain animals (Leviticus 11), but even a "clean" animal had to be slaughtered in a certain way, completely drained of blood, and prepared in a highly specific manner, since Hebrews were not permitted to taste fat, blood, or any meat cooked in milk (Leviticus 3:17; Deuteronomy 14:21). Such rules were absolutely binding on God's people at that time, designed in part to stress God's claim on every single part of life, even cooking and eating, and to assure that the people of God were measurably different from those who were not. Yet, how could Daniel explain this to the Babylonians? He would seem not only absurdly scrupulous, but what is worse, arrogant, insulting, and intolerant. Nevertheless, Daniel adopted a principle that is absolutely essential for those trying to follow God in a hostile or indifferent environment: He would not compromise God's Word.

The four were not being overly scrupulous. They knew the liberty they had through faith in the one true God. They were willing, for instance, to adopt Babylonian names whose meanings alluded to pagan deities (Daniel 1:7). Daniel's new name, Belteshazzar, means "May Bel protect his life." "Abednego" means "Servant of Nebo."[2] Bel and Nebo were idols, false gods; yet Daniel and Azariah took their names. Wasn't this rather liberal of them? Of course not. They knew that Bel and Nebo did not exist. They would not be harmed by a mere name, as long as it would not cause offense to those weak in their faith (cf. 1 Corinthians 8:4-10). The fifth day of the week we call Thursday, which means "the day of Thor." Midweek church services are announced for Wednesday, "the day of Wodan." Are we enmeshed in a Satanic web, unwittingly paying honor to pagan devil worship when we worship on Sunday, the day set aside for worship of the sun? Of course not. When we say Saturday, we are referring to the last day of the week. "Saturn" is part of the history of the word, its etymology, but has nothing to do with its present meaning, with the reality that the word refers to.

Christians should not be superstitious. Abject fear of pagan gods is little different from abject worship of them. Christians have been freed from all of that. Those who refuse to read Homer because he describes pagan gods or object to C. S. Lewis's The Lion, the Witch, and the Wardrobe, that

profound Christian masterpiece, because it has a witch in the
title and thus might be a point of entry for occult powers
should measure themselves by Daniel, Shadrach, Meshach,
and Abednego.

The dietary laws, though, were different. These set
them apart and gave them identity as people of God. They
were not willing to trade that identity away for the acceptance and prestige of Babylon. They had to ask themselves
what would govern their obedience and self-definition: the
king's table with its luxury, prestige, and social acceptance, or
the law of Moses with its austere demands. They had to make
a choice—to be assimilated into the dominant culture by
conformity or to remain distinctively different, remaining
aliens and outcasts. They resolved not to defile themselves.

There was probably another reason, besides the Mosaic
dietary laws, why the four rejected the king's table. The
atmosphere of the court no doubt also made them uncom-
fortable. God's people were nowhere forbidden to drink
wine, but Daniel here sees the king's wine as defiling also. No
doubt the court, like today's campuses and elite cocktail parties, was a place of general intoxication, where drunkenness,
hedonism, and luxurious excesses were the accepted pursuits
which preoccupied nearly everyone. Modern Christians are
often faced with the same atmosphere. One might be quite
ready to explain the principles of Biblical theism or to state
the grounds of one's salvation, but when it comes to turning
down the circulating marijuana cigarette, or making an issue
out of refusing to go to a pornographic movie, or rejecting
the elegant debauchery of a fraternity party, it is sometimes
much more difficult. A Christian, like Daniel, must refuse to
compromise the faith in even the smallest doctrinal or moral
principle.

PROBLEM SOLVING

And yet, Daniel was able to resolve the dilemma without
compromising his principles. Notice that the four do not turn
over the king's table, nor do they stand up and prophesy
publicly against Babylonians for eating pork. Rather, with
elaborate courtesy and respect, Daniel goes to the proper

authority: "therefore he asked the chief of the eunuchs to allow him not to defile himself" (1:8). It seems strange to ask permission to keep God's law, but this is what Daniel did.

As important as it was to avoid unclean food, Daniel understood the Biblical principle that he must respect all human authorities, even pagan ones (Romans 13:1-7), and that to avoid one sin, ritual defilement, by committing another one, rebellion, is to gain nothing. Biblical submission is a radical spiritual discipline. It embodies self-denial and faith in the sovereignty of God. To see God's authority looming behind all human authorities and to see in them how God employs secular governing for "your good" (Romans 13:4) is to acknowledge God's providence reigning over every part of life.[3] Daniel addressed these pagan authorities with courtesy and humility. He referred to himself and the other Hebrews as "your servants." He meant it. He wanted to serve them. As a result of his humility and his openness to authority, they could not help but like him.[4] Moreover, Daniel in his submission was being aided by the living God: "And God gave Daniel favor and compassion in the sight of the chief of the eunuchs" (1:9). The most hostile-seeming professor, administrator, or employer can be softened by the action of God.

Still, despite this God-given sympathy to their plight, the chief eunuch turned them down. The eunuch had an understandable concern: " 'I fear lest my lord the king, who appointed your food and your drink, should see that you were in poorer condition than the youths who are of your own age. So you would endanger my head with the king' " (1:10). If the four Hebrews did not seem as healthy as their Babylonian peers, the king would assume that the eunuch was not taking care of them as well as he should. Nebuchadnezzar's management style was not to fire ineffective employees but to cut off their heads.

Despite this initial setback, Daniel did not give up. He went to the next authority in the chain of command, the steward, and proposed a creative alternative:

"Test your servants for ten days; let us be given vegetables to eat and water to drink. Then let our

appearance and the appearance of the youths who
eat the king's rich food be observed by you, and
according to what you see deal with your servants."
So he hearkened to them in this matter, and tested
them for ten days. At the end of ten days it was seen
that they were better in appearance and fatter in
flesh than all the youths who ate the king's rich
food. So the steward took away their rich food and
the wine they were to drink, and gave them vegetables. (1:12-16)

Daniel's proposal addressed both sides. The authorities were
concerned with their health—that point must be preserved.
The Hebrews were concerned about the dietary laws. Is it
really true that they are forbidden to eat *anything* from a
Babylonian kitchen? What *can* they eat? Daniel realized that
the meat may not be kosher, but there is no reason why they
could not eat the vegetables, which are not covered by the
Mosaic code. They could thus still eat from the king's bounty,
avoiding giving offense, without violating their consciences.
As for the matter of their health, Daniel proposed a test, a
sort of controlled experiment to determine objectively
whether or not the chief eunuch's fear was well-founded.
Daniel was not afraid to submit himself to the facts.

Whether God was working a special miracle to sustain
their health, or whether Scripture is simply recognizing that a
vitamin-rich diet of vegetables is going to be healthier than
ten days of gourmet food, Daniel was vindicated. This was
not a one-sided triumph, however. The legitimate interests of
the authorities were maintained; the religious interests of the
Hebrews were also maintained, although in a nondisruptive
and sacrificial way—they do not demand kosher meat but are
simply willing to do without.

This is a model for any kind of conflict between Church
and State, or Christian versus non-Christian. Like Daniel, we
should first uncover any legitimate purpose behind the problematic issue. The licensing of religious schools may be intended simply to promote health and safety standards, which,
like Daniel, we should not oppose. The professor's assign-

ment to write a paper on a novel we find dangerously pornographic may be intended to increase one's understanding of
contemporary sexual attitudes. The roommate's offering a
marijuana cigarette may simply reflect a desire to become
friends, to form a social bond. The next step should be to
formulate an alternative. A Christian school might propose
compliance with state health standards and a Christian ac-
crediting agency rather than that of the state. Reading the
pornographic novel might be replaced by something else,
perhaps a study of the contemporary feminist critique of
pornography as degrading and enslaving to women. The
roommate could be shown by other friendly gestures that
friendship need not involve drugs.

The final step is, like Daniel, to submit to a test, showing the authority that the alternative is a superior way of
achieving the goal. If the state is concerned with academic
standards, the Christian school should offer a study of its
SAT scores. The Christian literature student who has refused
to read pornography should show that the alternative project
has shown that he or she understands contemporary sexuality very well—in fact, better and more profoundly than the
trendy Hugh Hefnerites. The Christian in the dormitory
should show that he or she can be a better friend to the
roommate than those whose friendship is based on something
as superficial as drugs.

Too often Christians do not react to conflicts in this
Biblical way. Christian schools file suit, students rage against
their teachers and refuse to turn in their assignments, room-
mates are shunned and condemned like Satan himself. As a
college English teacher, I have occasionally antagonized some
of my students for one reason or another. Very few took the
trouble to do as Daniel did, to approach me about it with a
view to resolving the problem. Of those few who have come
to my office, many of them were insufferable, displaying neither the humility nor the courtesy of Daniel. Students would
often want to find the easiest way possible, getting out of
assignments or finding shortcuts. Daniel, on the other hand,
went the route of self-denial, proposing to make it harder
upon himself.

TEN TIMES BETTER

Finally, the Bible describes the results of these three years in the University of Babylon: "As for these four youths, God gave them learning and skill in all letters and wisdom" (1:17). God gave them the learning. The Bible here clearly states that academic pursuits and accomplishments are not only pleasing to God, but that they are gifts which He bestows. "*All letters and wisdom*" come under the sovereignty and the gift of God, thereby sanctioning the whole range of human learning. Such all-inclusiveness gains even more force when it is remembered that the Scripture is referring to the knowledge of Babylon, a culture surely more ignorant of God, more immoral, than any modern university, which, as part of the Western intellectual tradition, has its origins at least in a Biblical world view.

In fact, their knowledge of the true God and of His Word gave the four an enormous advantage over the Babylonian intellectual establishment:

At the end of the time, when the king had commanded that they should be brought in, the chief of the eunuchs brought them in before Nebuchadnezzar. And the king spoke with them, and among them all none was found like Daniel, Hananiah, Mishael, and Azariah; therefore they stood before the king. And in every matter of wisdom and understanding concerning which the king inquired of them, he found them ten times better than all the magicians and enchanters that were in all his kingdom. (1:18-21)

In this final examination, God granted them success. Specifically, God's children, reared in the sophisticated intellectual climate of Babylon and also saturated with the truth of God's Word, proved themselves "ten times better" than their peers.

This should not be surprising. The Babylonian intelligentsia were brilliant and had many great scientific and mathematical accomplishments, but their erroneous world views and their pagan superstitions were a real obstacle to their pursuit of truth. The modern intellectual establishment is likewise impressive and accomplished, but it is also limited and hampered by its exclusion of Biblical truth. Scientists who only conceive of technique and technological mastery over nature, which they invest with divine qualities such as eternity and self-sufficiency, may be little different from the Babylonian "magicians." Artists who think they are creating meaning by their inspired aesthetic creations designed to please, mesmerize, and manipulate their audiences may be little different, really, from the Babylonian "enchanters."

What an advantage Christians should have, being freed from the credulities of secular humanism and the stifling limitations of scientific materialism. Christians may well prove themselves "ten times better than all the magicians and enchanters" who often dominate the academic world but are cripplingly ignorant of the truths that can only be found in God. Modern Christians, like Daniel, can likewise strive to meet modern thought on its own terms and to succeed and to exert their influence even in the modern-day Universities of Babylon.

What follows in this book is an attempt to show how that might be done. It is a stroll through some of the hanging gardens, a guide to the smorgasbord, the "King's Table," of the modern intellectual world. In it I try to suggest what might be nourishing and also what might be defiling. I also try to suggest why Christianity—pure, orthodox, and uncompromised—can, in fact, be a framework for knowledge of the widest scope and the most complex depths. I try to show how Christians might aspire like Daniel to be "ten times better" than their secularist counterparts.

PART TWO

THE MODERN MIND

FOUR

THE ATTACKS AGAINST CHRISTIANITY

Many Christians are not opposed to knowledge as such. They notice, however, that certain fields today make claims that do not always accord with what the Bible says. Biology involves the study of evolution. Psychology tends to either glorify human beings or trivialize them, leaving out the demands of God. The arts, although perhaps "Christian" four hundred years ago, today seem part of the worldly or even pagan mindset that Scripture warns against. What about purely secular fields of knowledge, such as science, technology, the humanities, or other areas that do not directly tie in to Christian thought? Might not a deep involvement in the modern intellectual scene, which often either ignores or opposes the revelation of God, be harmful to a person's faith?

These are serious, life-or-death questions. Many people do abandon their faith when they go off to college. Many Christians begin thinking that their earlier beliefs are narrow and limited compared to the exhilarating rush of knowledge they experience when they delve into modern psychology or when they find themselves accepted socially in the world of academia or the arts. They often then try to reconcile things that cannot be reconciled. If they retain a vestige of Christian beliefs, they feel constrained to reinterpret those beliefs in light of modern thought. They abandon the austere, all-consuming authority of the Bible but retain the parts they like. If their social and intellectual circles tolerate sexual immorality and abortion, they will make their theology similarly tolerant. If modern ideas conflict with the Bible, then it is the Bible that must be wrong.

One alternative to secularist education is Christian education. Christian schools exist at every level. At their best, they seek to integrate all of knowledge with the Christian faith. And yet, the secularist viewpoint can penetrate even Christian schools, colleges, and scholarship. To teach at a Christian college, one must have a graduate degree. Since there are few explictly Christian graduate schools, this means that even the Christian scholar must be proven and certified by the secular academic world. In my opinion, this is good—a Christian scholar should engage the modern intellectual world. The problem is, Christian scholars, to be accepted in their fields and to play a part in their professional disciplines, often find themselves thinking along the lines of their secularist colleagues, even when the academically respectable position conflicts with Christian orthodoxy. Thus, even students at Christian colleges are often scandalized by what they are learning. Christian students, Christian professors, and Christian professionals in every field must be aware of the contours of modern secularist thought.

The term *secular* means not religious, as opposed to *sacred*. There is a sense in which purely secular knowledge, that which involves no religious claims, may be the least problematic for a Christian. Water consists of two hydrogen atoms bonded to one oxygen atom—that fact has no religious content as such and would be acceptable to anyone of any faith or lack of faith. The problem is, what sometimes presents itself as secular is not secular at all. Statements about the meanings, origins, and purpose of life are intrinsically religious. Such sacred pronouncements from secular sources are what Christians need to be on guard against.

I believe that Christians can engage modern thought in a positive way without compromising their faith. They will, however, need to be aware of the specific attacks, temptations, and "sacred" ways of thinking that they will encounter. In this late twentieth century, Christianity is not in favor with the intellectual establishment. Christians need to understand that very clearly. Christians can learn from that establishment, and they can even take part in it—they are not shut out completely because of their faith and, as I hope to show, that faith can give them a real advantage. Still, Christianity will not make a person popular in academic circles.

ASSAILED FROM EVERY SIDE

G. K. Chesterton has observed how Christianity is attacked "on all sides and for all contradictory reasons."[1] He points out how some condemn Christianity for being too pessimistic, others for being too optimistic. Christianity is said to stress sin, judgment, and austerity, to be inhuman in its gloom and bleakness. Others, though, reject it for its pie-in-the-sky comforts. The belief in providence and a caring God, they say, hides the true bleakness and meaninglessness of life. The Church is ridiculed both for being antifemale and because in Europe only women still go to church. It is criticized for its austerity and for its extravagance, for being too peaceful and for being too violent. It is attacked because it lacks unity ("None of the churches agree with each other") and for being unified ("They don't allow differences of opinion").[2]

Such arguments are heard every day in classrooms, publications, and conversations. Followers of Karl Marx charge Christianity with suppressing the poor. Followers of Ayn Rand condemn Christianity for helping them. A person may accuse Christianity of being the opiate of the people and then, in the same conversation, complain about the Church's stand on drugs. Liberals hate Christianity for being conservative, and conservatives hate it for being liberal. One of my students ripped apart Christianity for being selfish and intolerant. Another student, a political conservative who had been reading Ayn Rand, attacked it for its altruism. According to him, selfish individualism is the highest good. Christianity's teachings of love and compassion have spoiled the free society.

In a history class, as Chesterton observes, Christianity might be blamed both for the ineffectual mildness of Edward the Confessor and for the ferocity of Richard the Lion-Hearted, for being too pacifist and for being too warlike. A science lecturer may snipe at Christianity for suppressing modern knowledge in the name of outdated superstitions. An anthropology teacher will then attack missionaries for introducing primitive cultures to modern technology and health-care. Some deride Christianity for being too rationalistic, reducing the mystery of life and the supernatural to a set of intellectual dogmas. Others dismiss it for being too emotional and mystical, an escape from reason into cloudy superstitions.

The point is not simply that the charges, taken together, contradict each other, but that Christianity is more complex, comprehensive, and whole than many of its critics realize. Chesterton provides the analogy:

> Suppose we heard an unknown man spoken of by many men. Suppose we were puzzled to hear that some men said he was too tall and some too short; some objected to his fatness, some lamented his leanness; some thought him too dark, and some too fair. One explanation . . . would be that he might be an odd shape. But there is another explanation. He might be the right shape. Outrageously tall men might feel him to be short. Very short men might feel him to be tall. . . . Perhaps (in short) this extraordinary thing is really the ordinary thing; at least the normal thing, the center.[3]

I do not intend to be glib. Many critiques of Christianity are strong and searching. They must be taken seriously. But many of the criticisms one encounters casually are glib— they are flippant and superficial, poorly thought out, and intended as cheap shots. The effect of such attacks on a Christian is not so much to give devastating intellectual challenges to one's faith but to wear a person down. One gets tired of all the abuse. Being on the defensive, especially against all fronts at the same time, can be emotionally draining.

Moreover, a person craves acceptance by peers and colleagues and teachers. Christianity seems to be the barrier. No one wants to be identified as one of the "fundamentalists" everyone is making fun of. No one wants to be seen as an enemy of earthly joys who refuses to see the meaninglessness of life, a suppressor of the poor and foe of the free enterprise system, a selfish, gullible, warlike pacifist. It is then easy to start resenting Christianity. One starts to accept, then to enjoy the petty objections that one hears. Soon it is easy to make petty objections of one's own.

Resisting such intellectual assaults is much like Daniel's rejecting the king's table. Personal ease and social acceptance must sometimes be sacrificed in a stubborn holding on to the fundamentals of the faith against all allurement, pressure, and mockery. Another help for the Christian is to have solid knowledge about what Christianity actually does teach.

IGNORANCE ABOUT CHRISTIANITY

Even some of the greatest, most distinguished scholars are often remarkably ignorant of what the Christian faith involves. The sophistication and knowledge present in modern culture is vast and rich; yet many people's view of Christianity is incredibly simple-minded. Here I am not referring to belief in Christianity, but simply knowing what it is that Christians believe.

To take an important example, it is commonly passed over that Christianity, as the name implies, involves Christ. Christianity is distinct among world religions, even Jewish and Islamic monotheism, in teaching that God became flesh in the historical Jesus. Yet, Christianity is continually made fun of for believing in a white-haired God in the sky, supremely aloof from human suffering. Or it is attacked for rejecting the physical world for some vague and cloudy spiritualism. Or the character of God is attacked for being too cold, judgmental, or absolutist.

Such charges are complex, of course. The problem of evil is indeed a problem. Christians do assert the importance of the spiritual realm and the absolute sovereignty of God. But surely the doctrine of the Incarnation, held by all Christians, complicates such charges in a profound way.

God is aloof from human suffering? The Christian God is a poverty-stricken Jew who was executed by torture. God in Christ entered the human world precisely to bear our griefs (Isaiah 53), to share in the suffering of human life.

Christianity rejects the material world? The Christian God is not a phantom but is manifest tangibly, in a human body of flesh and blood. When John speaks of the "Word of life," it is not some abstraction or a mystical experience but something "which we have seen with our eyes, which we have looked upon and touched with our hands" (1 John 1:1). Christianity, with its emphasis on incarnation, historicity, the value and significance of the physical world, might more logically be attacked for being "too materialistic," as indeed it is by apologists for other world religions.

God's personality is not attractive? Notice how almost no one, even the most militant atheist, will criticize the person of Jesus of Nazareth. They reject His deity, of course, and twist Him to suit their own beliefs—Marxists seeing Him as a political revolutionary, new-consciousness advocates seeing Him as an antiestablishment visionary—but nearly everyone holds Him up for the highest admiration.

This is highly unusual. Critics of Marxism think nothing of attacking Karl Marx. Antagonists of Mormonism readily discredit Joseph Smith. The founders of other philosophies and religions are not exempt from the *ad hominem* attack. One either agrees or disagrees with their teachings. Jesus, though, is different. I have never read anyone trying to refute the Sermon on the Mount. The only ones who present Jesus as a fraud or a psychopath are a few liberal theologians, with Nietzsche and Ayn Rand attacking Him more directly than most. Yet even they cannot hide their admiration for Him. Everyone pays at least some tribute to this Galilean carpenter whose effect, even among nonbelievers, is far different from any other human teacher. They cannot help but be "astonished at his teaching, for he taught them as one who had authority, and not as their scribes" (Matthew 7:28, 29). This has always seemed a great proof of the Christian faith, that Jesus is honored so universally. I do not even object much to the commercialization of Christmas. I love it when the secular world puts up tinsel and greenery and spends a great deal of money to celebrate the birthday of one whom they may not acknowledge but who is nevertheless their King and their Lord (Philippians 2:9-11).

This Jesus, whose personality all admire and whose teachings all praise, is the Christian God. Jesus is indeed sovereign and "judgmental," as portrayed in the four Gospels. In Him, though, such qualities are not objectionable. They seem fitting in Jesus, in harmony with His humility and love. The personality of God, for Christians, is manifest in the personality of Jesus, apart from whom we can know nothing about God (John 14:7). Our Heavenly Father is not as the critics usually portray Him—where are they getting this caricature? Rather, His personality and character is fully revealed in Jesus, and conversely the personality and character of Jesus is what Christians understand as the personality and character of God.

Another example of the general ignorance about Christian doctrine has to do with salvation. Many people, including many of Christianity's critics, assume that Christians believe that good people go to Heaven and bad people go to Hell. To go to Heaven a person must live a righteous life, which involves avoiding things that most people enjoy and striving by various means to reach God. If this is Christianity, it too is Christianity without Christ.

Christians, on the other hand, have always insisted that salvation comes from Christ and is offered to sinners. Although they differ in their understandings of exactly how that salvation is received, all Christians, Catholic and Protestant, have historically seen Christ as the source of salvation. Human beings do not come to God; God comes to human beings. Salvation cannot be purchased by good works, much less by good habits. It was purchased for us and on our behalf by the blood of Jesus Christ, the Second Person of the Trinity, who claims our sin and allows us to claim His righteousness. When we are united with Him, by grace through faith, He becomes our Savior.

This is far more complicated than the "good people go to Heaven, bad people go to Hell" theology, and it can certainly be criticized. It almost never is. The most severe critics of Christianity often know nothing of the central Christian concept of grace. Occasionally the basic concept of salvation by faith is criticized. In studying the complaints, however, it is apparent that the critics think Christians see faith as mere intellectual belief in abstract doctrines. Thus, salvation by faith becomes far more despised than salvation by works. They do not realize that Christians see themselves as being saved neither by faith nor works but by the grace of God (Ephesians 2:8). Grace is the love and the action of God, who in Christ calls us to Himself. Faith is acceptance and trust in what God has done for us. Good works are accomplished by God working in us as a result of faith. Both faith and good works are a response to and a gift of grace.

A good example of such misunderstanding can be seen in the most scholarly analyses of the Puritans. The term has become a synonym for austere moralism. Yet these people who are so often ridiculed for their strict morality were precisely the ones who most minimized the role of good works in salvation. Their strong emphasis on God's grace alone did bear fruit in moral action.

The concept of sin is likewise misunderstood, and not only by academic critics. I once gave a writing assignment that involved the students' exploring the topic of morality. Most of them, including many churchgoers, thought *sins* included such habits as smoking and drinking. Some did mention sex, but smoking and drinking were the sins that made up the great moral problems of our time. Now, not smoking and not drinking are rational, healthy practices, but these habits are not what the Bible means when it speaks of sin. My students had a hard time understanding the sense in which pride can be a "deadly sin." ("Pride? But Coach told us to have pride in ourselves, and our high school counselor hounded us to death if we didn't have a good self-image.") No one mentioned the Ten Commandments. (" 'Thou shalt not covet'? But what would happen to the economy if we didn't want what other people had?") The sense in which sin inheres in human nature, a twisting, ever-present perversion that lies in the hearts of all of us, no one noticed.

Chesterton has observed that the doctrine of original sin "is the only part of Christian theology which can really be proved."[4] Every utopia that has failed (why should they fail if human beings all want perfect peace and happiness?), every exalted human ideal that has been spoiled—and every utopia and every ideal has failed and has been spoiled—is evidence for the Christian doctrine of original sin.

It should not be possible for Christians to be disillusioned. We should have no illusions in the first place. Our faith is in Jesus Christ alone. When a human being disappoints us, when someone we admire turns out to be a hypocrite, when the Church itself proves corrupt, we should not be too surprised. This is our sinful condition. Christians know that there are no good people, that we are all lost, wallowing in our sins and capable of the most horrible actions, if not for the action of a Savior. When we realize this, it makes it much easier to forgive and to understand and to accept the sinner. This strain of Christian realism, tough-minded and compassionate at the same time, can give a Christian an important perspective on all of life.

DISILLUSIONMENT

If critics avoid attacking Christ, they are savage in their indictment of the Church. The accomplishments of the Church are overlooked, and Christian humility usually prevents the Church from standing up for itself. As evidence for the corruption of Christianity, critics will, for example, cite the Crusades and the Inquisition. (It is a strange sensation for Protestants, whose spiritual forebears suffered the stake, to find themselves blamed for the Inquisition.) Critics will cite example after example of brutality and hypocrisy on the part of Christians through the ages. Many of these criticisms are inaccurate and unfair, but grant them all.

The Church is a company of self-acknowledged sinners. That it can be bloody, brutal, obtuse, totalitarian, clumsy, and (what is perhaps worse to some people) vulgar is only another proof of its doctrine that "none is righteous, no, not one" (Romans 3:10). This is not to say that Christians should be complacent about impurity in the Church or hypocrisy in Christians. We should be its sternest critics and cling to the highest ideals as set forth in Scripture. However, failure to live up to these ideals—the occasions when Christians have been bloody, bigoted, and evil—cannot invalidate the Christian faith.

Many people who lose their intellectual grip on their faith do so because they become disillusioned. They still profess an admiration for Christ, but they start to reject institutional Christianity. They become aware of some of the shameful parts of the history of the Church—the pogroms, the Hundred Years' War, racial prejudice. Or, what can be even more devastating, they have had a bad experience in their own church. Their feelings have been hurt, they have been mistreated, they perceive hypocrisy in the staunch members of their church. The institutional Church acquires a bad connotation in their minds. They stop going to worship services. They start assuming that the great doctrines of the faith, including the Incarnation and the Redemption, are nothing more than mere dogmas of the Church. They drift farther and farther away, until their faith, which once may have been extremely ardent, dwindles to a memory, and then to a stage that they went through a long time ago.

I have seen this played out again and again in the lives of friends, colleagues, students, and scholars. Many of the fiercest enemies of Christianity often turn out to have been at one time devout Christians. Their bitterness is usually directly proportional to the hurt they received at the hands of other Christians.

No one can violently attack something without taking it seriously in some way. No one attacks belief in Zeus anymore. No one gets emotional over the Flat Earth Society. Yet Christianity calls forth the deepest emotions, even and especially in the ones who most reject it. The person who most vehemently condemns the faith may be closer to it than the cool agnostic who remains ignorant of it and blithely leaves it out of all consideration.

These hostile critics, tragically, are often "little ones" whom Christians have scandalized and caused to fall (Luke 17:1, 2). When Christians encounter such critics, they should not respond with hostility—much less try to make them lose their jobs. What good would that do? That would only confirm their disillusionment with Christians. Rather, Christians should obey Scripture and "bless them that curse you, do good to them that hate you, and pray for them which despitefully use you" (Matthew 5:44, KJV). Such behavior can be more eloquent than any argument, especially to someone who has been disillusioned by the behavior of Christians, and can go a long way in winning a brother.

In the meantime, Christians must fully understand the doctrine of sin so that they themselves do not become disillusioned. Offenses will indeed come (Matthew 18:7). Christians must take care not to be devastated by them. The doctrine of sin should ensure that they have no illusions to lose.

INFORM AND EXPLAIN

One of the best ways Christians can witness to our modern culture, both to the active enemies and to the far greater number of the ignorant and the indifferent, is simply to inform people objectively of what it is that Christians believe. It is usually not necessary to argue, to get drawn into deep esoteric discussions, or even to get defensive. Simply explain.

When Christianity is blamed for the Crusades, simply say, "I am a Christian, and our church does not require us to conquer the Holy Land." At one stroke it becomes clear that the Crusades are not the essence of Christian doctrine. When, in a literature class, Puritan Christians are ridiculed for being anti-art and anti-pleasure, simply raise a question: "What about Milton?" When a philosophy professor presents the problem of evil as disproving the existence of God (who if He is good and all-powerful would not permit human suffering), bring up Jesus Christ: "Christianity teaches that God became a human being in Jesus Christ and that He bore human suffering and sin on our behalf." That may not completely solve the problem, but it complicates it interestingly and at least sets the record straight. When the Church is criticized for being hypocritical, simply explain how Christianity is a religion that restricts itself to sinners. (This puts the critic in the awkward position of being self-righteous and judgmental, the very qualities he is criticizing in the Church.) When Christianity is attacked for rejecting physical reality, the ordinary pleasures of life, and human dignity, ask, "How can that be, when its central doctrines are that God created the world and was made flesh, coming into the physical world as a human being?"

Just as it is possible to explain what Buddhists believe, what Marxists believe, what existentialists believe, it is possible to explain what Christians believe. It can be done without proselytizing. It is not necessary to argue for these positions or even defend them. It is enough to state what they are. You can do this in a public school. It is not against the Supreme Court decisions. You are not asking anyone to believe in the Incarnation or the Redemption, but are simply explaining objectively what these terms mean. No one should object. No one would deny that these ideas are at least historically and culturally important and philosophically interesting.

Christians sometimes bring derision upon themselves and upon the faith by their loud and emotional sermons in the classrooms, by their defensive and belligerent accusations of "Blasphemy!" or "Satanic doctrine!" (What do you expect? You are in Babylon, not in church.) Witnessing does not mean being a witness for the prosecution. Nor is it primarily a statement of personal experiences, nor the outcome of a long, intellectual argument. Apologetics has its importance, but the gospel is not communicated by debates, by eloquent appeal, by personal charisma, by clever manipulation (1 Corinthians 1:18-25), but by the Word of God. When that Word, the message of Christ crucified, is presented, it is effectual and of itself can create faith in its hearers:

For the word of God is living and active, sharper than any two-edged sword, piercing to the division of soul and spirit, of joints and marrow, and discerning the thoughts and intentions of the heart. (Hebrews 4:12)

So faith comes from what is heard, and what is heard comes by the preaching of Christ. (Romans 10:17)

Daniel, the inspired prophet, bore God's Word into the courts of Babylon, a Word of Power that would later bring Nebuchadnezzar, the world conqueror with all of his authority and prestige, to his knees (Daniel 4). Modern Christians too, armed with Scripture, have that same power to uphold the truth against all attacks.

FIVE

THE EXCLUSION OF GOD

*I*t is usually not the specific arguments against Christianity that unsettle one's faith, but the whole atmosphere of modern thought. God is simply never factored in. Academic discussions of psychology, philosophy, science, humanities, even ethics and morality as a rule totally leave out of consideration the possibility that God might exist and have a bearing on the issues.

It seems sometimes that consideration of religious truth may be the one taboo of a permissive society. Flannery O'Connor wrote that the two things not allowed to be mentioned at the University of Kansas, my alma mater by the way, are whiskey and religion.[1] Today whiskey is acceptable on college campuses, but religion is still controversial. In a short story, one of O'Connor's characters exhibits this religious prudishness: "Jesus Christ in the conversation embarrassed her the way sex did her mother."[2]

This conspiracy of silence except for negative remarks makes one feel that religion is beneath the notice of serious pursuers of truth, that everything can be explained apart from any supernatural considerations.

SCIENTIFIC METHODOLOGY
Since the "Enlightenment" of the 1700s, scholars have insisted upon seeking explanations for observable events from within the closed natural order. Nature is considered a closed system. Anything that happens in nature must be accounted

for in terms of something else in nature. Any appeal to some supernatural realm outside the closed system is excluded automatically and by methodical rigor.

This methodology has obvious advantages. The prescientific mind could assert that it is raining because God was making it rain. That was enough. There was no thought of low pressure areas, cold fronts, movements in the atmosphere, and other factors that we now know cause it to rain. By looking at nature extremely closely, we can understand the exact mechanisms through which nature works.

The earlier view, however, is still correct. God does make it rain. The meteorologists are also correct. Theologians have always taught that God works through "secondary causes." God is the First Cause, who created and sustains the universe and who governs it as He wills. Secondary causes are the observable chain of events. Rain is caused by the condensation of water in the air due to a variety of chemical and climatic factors—the secondary causes. God is the First Cause of rain because He designed water, air, and the chemical processes that result in rain.

Modern science quite rightly focuses on secondary causes. The prescientific mind jumped to God too quickly, before the physical processes were fully analyzed and understood. There is no reason why people of faith cannot study these physical processes. To do so is to understand more fully what it is that God has done in His creation, to appreciate the created order in its full complexity and design, to see nature in depth as God created it.

THE DOMINANCE OF SCIENCE

The scientific methodology has permeated nearly all academic disciplines. Even disciplines that are not scientific as such— the arts, the humanities, philosophy, even theology—now make use of the scientific method. For example, in my freshmen composition classes I insist that abstract generalizations be grounded in concrete evidence and illustrated by tangible examples. This emphasis on evidence is part of the heritage of science and is found everywhere. It is valuable. An intellectual system needs some principle of verification. Insisting on concrete evidence makes for clarity, precision, and some assurance of truth.

At the same time, such a method imposes some limitations. If the test for truth is observable evidence only, that excludes some of the most interesting areas of life. Value judgments, ideals, and moral principles are not things that can be observed. They cannot be reduced to laboratory experiments. Certainly the assertion of spiritual realities, faith based on "the evidence of things not seen" (Hebrews 11:1, KJV), becomes almost impossible in these terms.

Instead of acknowledging that science is limited in its scope, that certain questions are outside the boundaries of science, the modern intellectual establishment will often assert naturalistic explanation in areas traditionally considered religious. The origin of the human race must be explained in terms of a series of natural causes—evolution by natural selection—not by reference to a supernatural Creator. The origin of the universe, even as evidence of a Big Bang is actually uncovered, may be analyzed in terms of mass and energy and complex mathematical calculations. But the possibility of a Creator, the traditional First Cause, must not even be mentioned.

The scientific methodology is especially clumsy when it comes to moral analysis. The social sciences go to great lengths to avoid value judgments. It always amused me how my sociology professors insisted that moral judgments are simply means of social control, that they are relative, situational, and not to be taken too seriously. They would then leave the classroom to protest American military involvements for being immoral. They were quick to label moral qualms about sexual practices or criticism of other cultures as only value judgments, but they could not avoid making such judgments themselves.

To the secularist mindset, moral issues must be resolved in terms of what is observable. Objective, authoritative absolutes which transcend the closed system of nature are excluded. For example, on the issue of abortion, orthodox Christians hold to the commandment, "Thou shalt not kill." This is an absolute, from which we infer the principle of the sanctity of life. We certainly make use of scientific evidence in showing that the fetus is a living, feeling, even thinking human organism. That human beings of whatever age or stage of development ought not to be killed simply because they are unwanted is a transcendent concept. Social expediency or human convenience can have no bearing on the absolute moral issues that are at stake.

The modern intellectual establishment proceeds in the opposite manner. Their concept of ethics must be based on observable social facts. There is a population problem, there are many unwanted children which add to the welfare rolls, pregnancies often interfere with the full emancipation of women, and so on. Therefore, abortion is an easy way to solve a host of social and personal problems. Moral absolutes can have no bearing on social expediency or concrete human happiness.

The same difficulties appear in questions of moral responsibility. If someone robs a convenience store (which is still a crime because it violates the security of a society), how are we to understand the crime and what should be done with the criminal?

Secularists must seek a reason for the criminal's behavior in terms of observable conditions, the closed natural system. Perhaps the criminal has been mistreated by the society and, as a result, is striking out against it. Maybe the cause can be found in the criminal's past—perhaps he was physically or emotionally abused as a child. Perhaps he suffered some trauma that made him commit the crime. If there is no evidence of such environmental problems, perhaps there is a physical reason. Perhaps there is some hormone imbalance or an abnormality of the brain or a genetic disposition towards antisocial behavior.

The idea that a person is a sovereign moral agent, free and self-determining and thereby responsible for his or her actions, whatever the complicating circumstances, is generally out of reach for many scholars. The controversy over whether human behavior is learned or genetic simply sets forth two different attempts to account for human complexities in terms of the closed natural system.

Both of them ultimately deny human freedom and dignity. This is the very boast of B. F. Skinner, the prestigious pioneer of behavioral science. In his book *Beyond Freedom and Dignity*, Skinner frankly argues that such notions are outdated and unscientific. Human beings can and should be manipulated for the good of them all.

To return to the criminal, it becomes difficult to see why he should be punished if he is not really responsible for his behavior. If crime is a sickness, it must be cured by hospitalization. If the criminal's problem is social maladjustment, he simply needs to be rehabilitated. This all sounds very humanitarian. But behind it lies the denial of the criminal's humanity. To quote Chesterton:

> That the sins are inevitable does not prevent punishment; if it prevents anything it prevents persuasion. Determinism is quite as likely to lead to cruelty as it is certain to lead to cowardice. Determinism is not inconsistent with the cruel treatment of criminals. What it is (perhaps) inconsistent with is the generous treatment of criminals; with any appeal to their better feelings or encouragement in their moral struggle. The determinist does not believe in appealing to the will, but he does believe in changing the environment. He must not say to the sinner, "Go and sin no more," because the sinner cannot help it. But he can put him in boiling oil; for boiling oil is an environment.[3]

Indeterminate sentences, manipulative psychology, rehabilitation as a mask for recidivism, prisons run by prisoners are, in fact, cruel and unusual punishment. The crisis in the modern criminal justice system and the failures of the prisons are testimonies to what happens when the concepts of moral responsibility and objective justice are rejected.

The scientific method is extremely valuable. This does not mean, however, that its particular assumptions, designed to study physical objects, can be carried over into every sphere of thought. When applied very strictly to human beings, the result is that human beings are reduced to merely physical objects, to animals, to machines. In arbitrarily excluding values, freedom, and the transcendent mysteries of the human life, such a view excludes everything of any importance, everything that makes someone human.

The intellectual assumptions of the scientific method are now even applied to theology. The result is the chain of circular reasoning that makes up much of modern liberal theology. Since only what is observable or according to natural processes can be accepted as valid, according to modern scientific methodology, the events described in the Bible must be demythologized. The Biblical text must be accounted for in terms of the closed, naturalistic system. If a book of prophecy predicts some historical event, that is taken to be evidence that the book was written after that event took place. Miracles simply do not happen in the "real" world. If a miracle is recorded in the New Testament, it must be a construction of the early Church, which must have compiled and developed the Gospel narratives over many, many years according to their theological needs. Traditional doctrines such as Heaven and Hell must be reinterpreted into visible, observable terms. Salvation becomes a metaphor for psychological counseling or political liberation.

The possibility of direct, supernatural inspiration as a means of knowledge cannot be taken into account by this view. The idea that an omnipotent, personal God exists who can break into history in miraculous ways is difficult for the modern mind. The thought that a realm of existence beyond the observable physical world is possible for human beings is dismissed as otherworldly.

The irony is that religion has always concerned itself with the supernatural, the unseen, the mysterious. In order to become intellectually respectable and accepted as a legitimate academic discipline, contemporary theology has often rejected its subject matter. Contemporary theology often ceases to be theology. Instead, it becomes psychology, sociology, philosophy, or politics. The supernatural is excluded in favor of naturalistic explanations to the point that theology must by its very methodology rule out God.

Theology was once considered "the Queen of the Sciences," the discipline that gave the foundation and meaning to all other forms of knowledge, unifying them all. Now the physical sciences have become Queen, to the point of limiting, restricting, and setting the ground rules for all other disciplines.

It is not criticizing the physical sciences to insist that the assumptions and methods of that discipline are not always applicable to human beings, the arts, philosophy, or religion. Just as it was absurd in the Middle Ages to apply the methods of scholastic theology to the study of physical nature, so it is absurd today to apply the rules of scientific analysis to the study of theology.

Albert Einstein observed that science can help human beings attain their goals; science cannot, however, supply the goals.[4] If we desire to feed the world, science can help us to do so. If we decide to exterminate the world, science can help us to do that also. Science, though, as a method and as a field of knowledge is simply unable, by its very nature, to make the decision for us. Many people assume that what is scientifically possible is always desirable. Einstein would disagree. What is possible and what is desirable involve two separate realms of knowledge. Whether to abort a fetus or to save a fetus's life through high-tech surgical techniques are not questions science can answer for us.

Einstein goes on to observe that "Perfection of means and confusion of goals seem—in my opinion—to characterize our age."[5] We have the means to do almost anything, but we are paralyzed because we do not know what to do. Although we are far advanced scientifically, we are extremely primitive morally. We can control nature, but we cannot control ourselves. It is with what Einstein calls the setting of goals that theology and the humanities have always been concerned. Why are human beings here? How should we act towards one another? What is necessary for happiness? What is the purpose of life? Such issues of goals, ideals, and purpose are real in every sense of the term. The assumptions of the physical sciences should not prevent such questions from being asked or answered.

MYTHOLOGIES AND SCHEMA-TESTING

Modern theorists, considering the discoveries of the new physics and recent studies of how human beings derive and formulate knowledge, are coming to realize that the scientific model has its limitations. It is not purely objective or value-free. The scientist cannot escape making assumptions according to some world view or making personal, partially subjective interpretations. Mechanistic views of the human being are currently being shown to be inadequate, as the failures of many of the educational, psychological, and social engineering experiments are making clear. Today is an exciting time in academia. It is a time for schema-testing, for reassessing methodologies, for rethinking what we know and how we know it.

Christians need to participate in this schema-testing. They see things from a perspective that is much needed in modern thought. They should not fear the scientific method, but they should see its limits. Like Daniel, they need to recognize mythologies.

A mythology is an imaginative model that helps to explain the natural world. In ancient Babylon, the stories of Marduk and Ishtar helped to explain the agricultural cycles and the motions of the stars. They were based on observable facts, and they were very functional—one could predict eclipses and plant and harvest crops with the aid of the mythology. In this sense, science is a "mythology." It provides models to help us explain and manipulate our environment. These models were formed by highly imaginative and intuitive human beings, and they are capable of being changed as new data is discovered.

At one time, scientists formulated the Ptolemaic view of the universe, that the sun and the planets circulate around the earth. This model was empirical—that is, after all, exactly what we see—and it was worked out with the most rigorous mathematics. With the invention of the telescope and new observations of the universe, a new model was put forward. The Copernican model, that the earth revolves around the sun, was radical. It went against what we actually observe and all sensory data, violating common sense and flying in the face of what everyone can see every morning—the sun rising above the horizon. This schema-testing, the replacing of one model of thinking with another, was met with furious opposition, as new models always are, but it explained the more subtle observations more thoroughly and eventually it was accepted. Today Einstein's notions of the relationships between space and time, the mechanics of light and gravity, and such corollaries as quasars and black holes fly in the face of common sense more than ever, and yet they give us an even more complete accounting of the data.

Those who see science as yielding unchanging truth should study the history of science and ask themselves one other question: If science has given us a series of models to explain the ever-increasing data, do we expect what science tells us now to be absolute? In one hundred years, will science be telling us the same thing that it is telling us today? Won't the models change, as they have always changed in the past? If the science of 1500 seems rather primitive and naive, won't our science also seem primitive and naive in five hundred years? What science proclaims as fact is not always so certain to the next generation of scientists.

If modern science is a "mythology" in a sense, it is far superior to the Babylonian mythology. The scientific method is much more sophisticated, more reliable, and more secular. In many ways, the secular quality of modern science is exactly what can most commend it to modern Christians. The Babylonians saw nature, their social life, and the gods as being all interconnected. Again, modern science arose when the Bible insisted that there is only one God who transcends His creation. The prophets' insistence that nature and society are not sacred opened up the world to human inquiry and innovation.

Insofar as science is objective and secular—that is, not pretending to offer values or explanations that are the province of religious faith—it is to be prized and celebrated. When someone tries to make it into a religion, as often happens with any mythology, science itself must affirm that such a role is out of its range, limited as it is to the observable and the empirical. It is quite a different thing to suggest that the observable and the empirical are all that can exist, that values and the spiritual realm must be fictions. That would be a religious claim, not a scientific one. It is to blur the scientific and the religious realms just as the Babylonians did.

Christians need not fear facts but should pursue them to their ultimate source. Christians can participate in the sciences and in the schema-testing that is underway at this very moment. In science, physical evidence—the remnants of energy fields and the motions of the galaxies—is pointing to an actual moment of creation. The universe is finite. There was a time when it did not exist. Theories of relativity, data on subatomic particles, and the calculations of quantum physics are pointing to a universe that is more baffling, more spiritual than anyone had dreamed. Mechanistic logic—the source of the old nineteenth-century materialism—is no longer adequate to account for such things. Scientists are no longer necessarily materialists.

In other fields, a scientific insistence upon evidence can demystify many political ideologies and psychological theories. Many of these simply do not work and do not account for the facts. Christians can benefit from the skepticism fostered by modern academia, if they can remember to sometimes apply that same skepticism to modern academia itself.

SIX

TRADITIONALISTS AND PROGRESSIVES

*T*here seem to be two different styles or emphases in the intellectual world today. Each has different values. Each will attack Christianity in a different way. At the same time, each can support Christianity in a different way.

A university, for example, has two functions. It first must preserve the accumulated knowledge and experience of the civilization and transmit that heritage to future generations. This is its traditionalist function. Without it, every generation must start over again from nothing. Knowledge builds on itself, so that today we stand on a pyramid of past discoveries. And yet, the weight of the past, the vast body of received learning, could well stifle and prevent new knowledge. There must also be an element of resistance to the past, of questioning and rethinking, so that new ideas can add to and change the edifice of the past. There must also be a progressive function. Without it, we would be satisfied with what we already know, or think we know, and inquiry, curiosity, and research would cease.

Both the traditionalist and the progressive functions are extremely important and valuable. Although they seem to be opposites, they are complementary. They exist in tension but in harmony at the same time. In a university, some professors will be traditionalists. Others will be progressives. Some scholars will have elements of both. A good university needs to contain both styles. For Christians, each contains a certain risk and a certain promise. Christians with a Biblical faith can be both traditional and progressive.

TRADITIONALISM

The traditionalist tends to focus on the great monuments and movements of the past, seeing them as testimonies of human achievement, as essential parts of the human heritage. The philosophical thinking of Plato, the richness of medieval symbolism, the plays of Shakespeare, the wit of Voltaire, the brilliance of Einstein—these are indeed great treasures, worthy of study and of being shared with every succeeding generation. If these were no longer read, understood, or transmitted, if they were lost, the whole human race would be poorer.

This perspective is perhaps the most sympathetic to Christianity. Even the most bitter atheist must acknowledge that Christianity has been a major force and influence in Western civilization. There are scholars who personally reject Christianity but are experts in Christian doctrine and civilization. Their expositions of theology as it relates to literature, art, and culture are often exhilarating, even inspirational. Christianity is part of the "Tradition." As such, it demands respect and serious study.

In colleges, Christian professors do exist. In fact, students may be surprised how many they are and how often they turn up. They are very important allies to Christian students in the midst of Babylon. Such Christian professors are often of the traditionalist party. They sometimes confuse evangelical students, however.

Many Christian academics, for example, tend to be attracted to historical denominations, Churches that have been an important part of the Western tradition as it has developed through the centuries. They tend to be attracted to ritual, to a liturgical mode of worship, and to sacramental theology. Such worship seems timeless, a way of uniting in a meaningful way with Christians throughout the ages. Ancient forms, practices, and doctrines are kept alive in the present, which theologically may seem superficial compared to the rich spirituality of the past.

Thus, many of the Christian traditionalists in academia will be Roman Catholics. The Protestants in their number tend to be Episcopalians. They may show some impatience with modern evangelicals who sometimes lightly ignore the Church's historical dimension. To traditionalists, many evangelicals seem extremely modern in their emphasis on self and on emotionalism. Many Christian academics come close to commiting assault and battery on their evangelical students who ask hopelessly simple-minded questions: "But was St. Francis of Assisi a *Christian?*" "Exactly when did Milton come forward at an altar call to accept Jesus Christ as his personal Lord and Savior?" "If Bunyan was really such a good Christian, why didn't he pray in faith so that God would let him out of prison?"

Objections to evangelicals on the part of traditionalists are often unfair. (However, when I was asked the question about Bunyan, who was imprisoned for his faith during which time he wrote *Pilgrim's Progress,* I did not take it calmly.) Still, there is often some truth to them. There is superficiality in the modern evangelical world. Many Bible-believing Christians share the modern taste for self-gratification, emotionalism, and anti-intellectualism. Many people who believe in the Bible have never read it. Evangelicals need to understand the point of such criticisms and to let their faith deepen and mature. Despite such quarrels, traditionalists will often be the evangelicals' closest allies. They will nearly always respect orthodox Christian positions more than liberal ones.

On the other hand, traditionalism can lend itself to problems from a Biblical perspective. Traditionalists sometimes confuse religion with culture. They are tempted to evaluate theology in terms of cultural or even aesthetic standards. That the Middle Ages enjoyed a unified, ordered vision of the world is not evidence that their religious system was at all points theologically correct. The artistic glories of the Vatican are no arguments for the primacy of the Pope. Traditionalist Christians sometimes look to human accomplishments and human institutions more than to the Word of God.

As for the non-Christian traditionalists, they criticize

Biblical Christians for being too narrow and ascetic. They fault us for tying salvation too exclusively to Christ. "What about Socrates?" they ask—"What about the glories of the ancient Chinese civilization? Did they have no religious wisdom? Were they all damned?" To them, Christians tend to undervalue our Greek and Roman heritage. We do not sufficiently appreciate the arts. We sometimes oppose other cultures. We are narrow-minded.

It is important, though, for Christianity to maintain its inherent radicalism. Christianity is not simply another cultural institution. Christianity is sometimes assimilated by the culture and turned into simply another mythology which exists to give a divine aura to human institutions.[1] The Bible makes clear that all such institutions—cultures, laws, political systems, works of art, human authorities—stand under the judgment of God. Human culture and institutions are valuable. They are God's gifts to human beings, who, created in God's image, have incredible powers and responsibilities and who are capable of remarkable accomplishments. Still, we are not to worship our own creations. For the Babylonians, culture and religion were identical. To oppose the king was to oppose the gods. Daniel's rejection of this idea, his refusal to pray to the king, brought him to the den of lions (Daniel 6).

Jesus enjoins us to render "to Caesar the things that are Caesar's, and to God the things that are God's" (Matthew 22:21). Both realms are thereby opened to the Christian. Both realms are also kept distinct. When the things of God and the things of Caesar are confused with each other, both realms are endangered. Human kingdoms are not holy in themselves. Caesar must not be worshiped. By the same token, what is holy must not be identified with the human kingdom. The Church may not rule politically. Christianity must not be turned into another civil religion. If the Church becomes indistinguishable from a particular culture, it loses even its influence on that culture.

Although traditionalists perform a good service in preserving the values and the ideas of the past, which includes Christianity, they should beware of slipping into idolatry. The Bible defines idolatry as worshiping and serving the creature instead of the Creator (Romans 1:25). Put another way, it involves basing one's faith on human creations, however noble they may be, rather than upon the Word of God.

Many of my colleagues and friends use the great texts and artifacts of our civilization exactly as Christians use the Bible. When seeking guidance, or when faced with some difficulty, or when looking for answers to life's questions, they turn to Shakespeare or Whitman or Yeats. They treat these great poets as authoritative and absolute. Shakespeare indeed conveys great meaning and profound ideas. Often his writings are saturated with Scripture. Still, it is vital to remember that Shakespeare's works—even with the large numbers of concordances, commentaries, and quasi-theological controversies that they have brought into being—are the words of a man, not the Word of God.

Traditionalists must be careful lest "for the sake of your tradition, you [make] void the word of God" (Matthew 15:6). They must not "hold fast the tradition of men" in such a way that they "leave the commandment of God" (Mark 7:8). When this distinction is kept in mind, however, traditions and the words and works of human beings through the ages can be valued in their proper place.

PROGRESSIVISM
Universities exist not only to conserve and perpetuate the knowledge of the past. They also exist to question that knowledge, to develop new ideas and revolutionary technologies. This is the function of progressivism.

Skepticism is an important intellectual tool. Accepted wisdom and tried and true answers must be subjected to critical scrutiny. New discoveries must always be searched for. Otherwise, the intellectual venture stops. Progressives emphasize the dynamic process of learning. They stress the changes in knowledge, the reinterpretation of evidence, the discovery of new facts and new hypotheses to explain them. Progressives are probably the most scathing critics of Christianity, which they tend to see as one of the old ideas they seek to discredit. Still, Christians can learn from them and can even adopt their methods in a Biblical way.

Progressives, by their very nature, tend to be opposed to traditional religions such as Christianity. They prefer revolutionary creeds such as Marxism. Interestingly, part of their problem with Christianity is their hostility to static dogma. Christianity purports to be a revealed religion, asserting absolute truths found in Scripture. For many progressives, accepting such a religion would be intellectual suicide. They do not reject it because its doctrines may not be well-founded—progressives do not think much of static logic either. For them, any final answer, the very principle of accepting any truth as absolute and final, shuts off the free inquiry of the mind, putting an end to the questioning and the searching which they see as the sum of the intellectual life.

Many progressive theologians, such as Paul Tillich, have gone further, insisting that questioning and searching is the sum of the spiritual life. For them, any final answers, including those asserted by classical Christian orthodoxy, are idolatrous. The life of faith is characterized by openness and uncertainty. Traditional defenses of Christianity which are designed to prove that Christianity is true will have little impact on people with this mind-set.

Another antirational tendency of progressivism is what C. S. Lewis terms "chronological snobbery."[2] In this view, anything new is preferred over anything that is old. Ideas are evaluated not according to logic or evidence but by the calendar. New or fresh ideas are assumed to be innately superior to old or traditional ideas. The worse thing that can be said about any idea is that it is outdated. If anything is labeled avant garde, or the wave of the future, or revolutionary, or modern, or, better yet, post-modern, it will be accepted not only uncritically but almost naively.

By logic, an idea must be either true or false (or qualified as partially true or partially false). The time frame in which the idea was formulated can have nothing to do with its validity. As Chesterton has observed, an abstract idea cannot be true on Monday and false on Tuesday. That the most recent ideas can hardly have been tested or scrutinized very thoroughly, or that the test of time is the most rigorous of tests does not occur to many progressives.

Thus, the divinity of Christ is dismissed as a third-century Hellenic notion. The Ten Commandments are minimized as reflecting an early stage of moral development. Belief in God is criticized as a primitive superstition. That their image of Christ as a revolutionary guerrilla and their belief in situation ethics are so flagrantly determined by the time in which they live, with its particular fashions and trendiness, does not matter too much to progressives. At its most superficial, progressivism involves the same mind-set encountered by Paul in the Athenians, who "spent their time in nothing except telling or hearing something new" (Acts 17:21).

Yet, there is a sense in which the skepticism, iconoclasm, and revisionism of the progressives can be especially congenial to the Christian. Perhaps even more so than traditionalism.

To be sure, Christians must remember that "Jesus Christ is the same yesterday and today and for ever" (Hebrews 13:8). With the eternal God "there is no variation or shadow due to change" (James 1:17). Nor does the moral law change (Matthew 5:17-19). Nor does God's Word (Deuteronomy 12:32; Revelation 22:18, 19). Liberal theology and the "new morality" have little to offer to an orthodox Christian.

The Bible stresses, though, that just as God is absolute and eternal, the human order and even the created order *are* transitory:

A voice says, "Cry!"
And I said, "What shall I cry?"
All flesh is grass,
and all its beauty is like the flower of the field.
The grass withers, the flower fades,
when the breath of the LORD blows upon it;
surely the people is grass.
The grass withers, the flower fades,
but the word of our God will stand for ever.
(Isaiah 40:6-8)

Heaven and earth will pass away, but my words will not pass away. (Mark 13:31)

God's Word does not change, but everything else does.

To insist that God's Word is absolute is not to insist that all knowledge is absolute. On the contrary, a high view of Scripture holds that human knowledge, apart from God's Word, is fallen, limited, and partial ("for our knowledge is imperfect. . . . Now I know in part . . ." [1 Cor. 13:9, 12]). Human institutions, governments, laws, monuments, religions, customs are all under the judgment of God and will "pass away." Daniel himself is given a vision of such great scope that it encompasses the rise and fall of civilizations, all of which are shattered by the Rock that is Christ (Daniel 2:31-45).

Christians can and must subject any human creation and institution to the most skeptical and critical scrutiny. They dare not make anything made by sinful human beings into a sacred absolute. The progressive function is thus open to Christians in a profound way.

Herbert Schneidau argues that the openness of Western civilization to change, its refusal to accept institutions or ideas as eternal, the very spirit of critical inquiry nourished by our intellectual heritage, is due directly to the influence of the Bible.[3] Mythological cultures, says Schneidau, are fully integrated and sanctioned by their religious systems. In Babylon the king was divine; the laws of the society were the same as the laws of the gods; the economic and social life of the people was regulated by their religious castes and cycles. In such societies, it is literally impossible to criticize the government. There is not even the concept of a transcendent moral law by which to judge the king and his laws.

Such societies are remarkably resistant to change when left to themselves. Certain tribes of New Guinea are still today practicing the ways of their Stone-Age ancestors. Their "mythological" cohesiveness allows them to be this conservative. Jericho, the world's oldest city, stood for thousands of years, a static never-changing monument of human, mythological conservatism until its walls were blasted by Joshua's trumpets.

In contrast, our Western culture has changed enormously in a mere two thousand years, in a mere century, in a decade. The reason, says Schneidau, is the Bible. For societies touched by the Bible, it is impossible to believe that the government is sacred, that the society is holy. Human institutions may not pass themselves off as divine. There is a moral law that transcends the social system. Even the king must obey the Law of God. The one God alone is eternal and holy. Everything else, being transitory, changes; and when it conflicts with the Law of God, it must be changed.

There is nothing like that in non-Biblical cultures. When the prophets denounced the idols of the Canaanites and insisted that the worshipers of the one God must never conform to the ways of the mythological cultures that surrounded them, when they insisted that the king of Israel himself must change his ways or suffer the wrath of God, they were establishing critical thinking, iconoclasm, and active change as a vital part of the Western mind.[4]

Believers of the Bible can therefore be progressives, not by rejecting Biblical absolutes, but precisely by applying them to human culture. God's Word has a caustic, corrosive effect on idols of all kinds. Any human pretensions to having captured absolute truth—whether a scientific model, a philosophical system, a historical interpretation, or a political program—fall short when exposed to the radical critique offered by Scripture. It is easy for monuments of the past or cultural practices, although valuable in their limits, to be turned into idols. The prophets and iconoclasts of the Bible are models for an important function of the intellectual life, and Christians can follow their example in criticizing accepted ideas and opening up the edifice of knowledge to revision and change.

As a matter of fact, Christians of today are especially called to play this role. Although there was a time when Judeo-Christian assumptions were the established viewpoint, to be challenged by progressives, today the situation is exactly reversed. Scientism, materialism, existentialism, and nihilism make up the intellectual establishment today. These movements, once radical and shocking, are now the orthodox, commonly accepted positions. Christians are now the heretics. They are the outsiders, the ones who must raise questions and challenge the prevailing orthodoxies.

In theology, art, and many other spheres of knowledge, the rebels have captured the citadel. Although they persist in calling themselves revolutionaries, they have become as repressive, dogmatic, narrow-minded, and hostile to change as their old opponents. Today an academic who doubts evolution, who rejects moral relativism, who does not mouth the pieties of secular humanism often faces violent and outraged opposition. That person stands, though, where the true progressive has always stood, outside the circle of accepted thinking. From this vantage point, new ideas become possible and the circle of knowledge can be made to expand.

SEVEN

THE MORAL ISSUES

Christianity is criticized from many different angles and for many different reasons. Beneath the intellectual issues, however, is something much deeper. Just as rational arguments alone are not sufficient to lead someone into faith in Jesus Christ, rational arguments are probably not enough to lead someone to reject faith in Jesus Christ. The Bible says that the real cause of unbelief is sin.

Human nature is so deformed by sin that our very capacity to reason, to discern, and to act on truth is distorted. Our problem is deeper than mere ignorance of the facts, a mental lapse, or a sincere misunderstanding. We are dead in our sins. No one can be brought into the faith by reason alone—our minds will run and hide from the reality of God. Rather, we must be altogether changed by the Holy Spirit, who brings us to faith in Christ through the gospel. By the same token, a person who rejects Christ does not do so merely because of intellectual analysis. The conviction of the mind is certainly important in both cases, but even more essential is the conviction of sin.

Christians trying to keep their equilibrium in a hostile world need to realize this, both to understand why their arguments so often have little effect and to be on guard lest their own faith be eroded in a way they do not expect. Sometimes convinced Christians are quite able to defend their faith in intellectual terms, but they are less able to defend themselves and their faith against moral temptations, which can often be far more caustic to their relationship with God than any ideas they may encounter.

Today the problem may be more subtle than in the past. Then, people sinned with abandon as they always have, but they at least acowledged that their behavior was sinful. Today the very concept of individual morality is challenged. There is still a great deal of moral zeal and even self-righteousness, but it tends to be projected out into the periphery of human control, focusing on social issues rather than personal ones. The world, the flesh, and the Devil, our old enemies, seem to have a special allure today, sometimes disguising themselves as virtues. Christians who become involved in the mainstream of modern thought need to understand very clearly the moral contours of contemporary culture and the spiritual dynamics of sin and unbelief.

SIN AND UNBELIEF
"He who is estranged seeks pretexts to break out against all sound judgment" (Proverbs 18:1). According to this text, a person first becomes "estranged"—that is, a close relationship is broken, so that love is replaced by hatred or indifference. The person who is estranged then looks for "pretexts"—excuses, rationalizations, arguments, and other masks which cover up the real problem. The person uses these "pretexts" to "break out" against the truth. This is evident in our relationships with other people. When friends hurt our feelings, their objective faults, which never bothered us before, stand out in glaring clarity. It is also true in our relationship with God. When we become "estranged" from God (that is, when we sin), we often start to manufacture a whole range of excuses by which we can "break out" against the truth of His Word. In fact, there seems to be a pattern of unbelief, a cycle that can be seen in the lives of many unbelievers. It goes something like this:

A young man is raised in a Christian home and has some measure of belief in Christ. He then becomes involved in some sort of overt sin. This can be any sin—pride, covetousness, addiction, dishonoring of parents, worldliness. It is often a sexual sin. He has the honesty and presence of mind to realize that this favorite sin is incompatible with the Christian faith. He has the moral sensitivity to experience guilt.

There are two ways he can respond. He may repent of the sin and turn to Christ to receive full and free forgiveness. Or he may hold on to the sin, treasure it, and refuse to give it up either overtly or emotionally. He starts to center his life around the sin, to seek from it consolation, help, and escape, to find in it, in effect, the meaning of his life.

But what about the guilt? If he is not interested in repenting and being forgiven, then there is only one way to end the torment: to reject whatever it is that brands his life as evil. If what I am doing is not really wrong, then I can "feel good about myself." If there is no objective standard of right and wrong, I can do as I please. If there is no God, then I am not a sinner.

At this point, the "pretexts" are discovered. There are many reasons not to believe in God. They become extremely persuasive to someone who wants to disbelieve. The arguments with the most force become those which turn one's own moral failures against their Judge, so that one's own sinfulness is projected onto God Himself: "I can never believe in God because He allows so much evil in the world." God becomes imagined not as the source of good, but as the source of evil. This moral crusade becomes directed against Christians in general—a narrow-minded, intolerant, hypocritical lot—and against the Church in particular. This moral zeal creates a feeling of self-righteousness, a precious feeling to those who have been tormented by guilt.

But his confidence is not totally secure. The very smell of Christianity or the very mention of Jesus Christ triggers his defenses. He lashes out at anything or anyone that represents the old belief which is still so accusing. He "breaks out" with startling emotion and aggressiveness against something which, supposedly, he does not even believe exists. He may lose himself in humanitarian causes. He may develop new theologies. He may become one of those professors in a university who delights in tearing down his students' faith. But there is a presence that will not go away, something looming in the background which he must always either fight against or give in to.

This psychological pattern can be broken at any point by the Word of God, by the devastating truth of God's Law and the penetrating grace that is offered in the gospel of Jesus Christ, who died to save sinners. The unbeliever is not playing an intellectual game, but is caught up in the complex spiritual dynamics of sin at war with the love of God. For a Christian, this pattern illustrates the slippery slope of unrepented and rationalized sin.

SUPPRESSING THE TRUTH

In the first chapter of Romans, St. Paul further analyzes the relationship between sin and unbelief as it applies more broadly to the intellectual scene of his day and of our own:

> For the wrath of God is revealed from heaven against all ungodliness and wickedness of men who by their wickedness suppress the truth. For what can be known about God is plain to them, because God has shown it to them. Ever since the creation of the world his invisible nature, namely, his eternal power and deity, has been clearly perceived in the things that have been made. So they are without excuse; for although they knew God they did not honor him as God or give thanks to him, but they became futile in their thinking and their senseless minds were darkened. Claiming to be wise, they became fools, and exchanged the glory of the immortal God for images resembling mortal man or birds or animals or reptiles. (Romans 1:18-23)

Wickedness suppresses the truth (1:18). "Whatever is true," says St. Paul elsewhere, we are to "think about" (Philippians 4:8). Christians never have to fear anything that is true, but they do need to fear sin. Sin can not only wreck a person spiritually, but also intellectually. Sin is anti-intellectual.

The passage points out that our rebellion against God is

not due to a lack of knowledge, even for the hidden tribes-
men of New Guinea who have never heard of the Bible.
Because of the creation—our having been created in the
image of God and our experience with God's creation—we
do know our Creator. The problem is, we refuse to "honor
him as God." When God the Creator is excluded, our very
thinking becomes "futile." Our minds, designed to understand the creation, become "senseless," "darkened." Yet, this
very point of mental blindness is when we "claim to be wise."
We transfer our allegiance from the immortal God to things
that are as mortal as we are. We reject God and turn to things
that are less than God. Not wanting to honor anyone higher
than ourselves, we honor what is human, or even less than
human ("birds or animals or reptiles").

God punishes this rebellion in a horrible way. He lets us
do what we want:

> Therefore God gave them up in the lusts of their
> hearts to impurity, to the dishonoring of their bod-
> ies among themselves, because they exchanged the
> truth about God for a lie and worshiped and served
> the creature rather than the Creator, who is blessed
> for ever! Amen. For this reason God gave them up
> to dishonorable passions. Their women exchanged
> natural relations for unnatural, and the men like-
> wise gave up natural relations with women and were
> consumed with passion for one another, men com-
> mitting shameless acts with men and receiving in
> their own persons the due penalty for their error.
> And since they did not see fit to acknowledge God,
> God gave them up to a base mind and to improper
> conduct. They were filled with all manner of wick-
> edness, evil, covetousness, malice. Full of envy, mur-
> der, strife, deceit, malignity, they are gossips, slan-
> derers, haters of God, insolent, haughty, boastful,
> inventors of evil, disobedient to parents, foolish,
> faithless, heartless, ruthless. Though they know
> God's decree that those who do such things deserve
> to die, they not only do them but approve those
> who practice them. (Romans 1:24-32)

God punishes us by letting us sin. He gives us up to the lusts of our hearts. This is indeed a stern judgment. The more we sin, the more degraded and corrupt we become. Estrangement from God leads to confusion of mind—to preferring lies to truth, to false religions, to "futile thinking" that has the illusion of wisdom. This estrangement, this primal sin, leads in turn to overt immoral behavior—homosexuality, murder, heartlessness, and other evil actions and desires.

St. Paul shows us that we have no excuse (Romans 2:1), that all cultures and all individuals are part of this network and conspiracy of sin and unbelief, this vicious circle from which no one can escape, except that God Himself has provided the remedy: "For there is no distinction; since all have sinned and fall short of the glory of God, they are justified by his grace as a gift, through the redemption which is in Christ Jesus, whom God put forward as an expiation by his blood, to be received by faith" (Romans 3:22-25).

INDIVIDUAL MORALITY AND SOCIAL MORALITY

For St. Paul, it is one thing to commit the sins which he lists; what is even more perverse is to approve of them (Romans 1:32). We poor sinners may be caught up in the bondage of the sins he describes, but if we at least acknowledge that they are wrong, we can repent and receive forgiveness. What is monstrous to St. Paul is that we can come to the point of actually "approving" such things, of saying that there is nothing wrong with homosexuality, murder, heartlessness, and the rest. When we justify such behavior in ourselves or others, we make repentance and deliverance impossible. What St. Paul is indicting is the sort of moral tolerance now widely extolled as one of the benefits of the educated mind.

Tolerance may be one of the few personal virtues still prized and demanded by many academic and professional circles. The stigma against sexual immorality has long since vanished. Extramarital sex has become the norm, so that chastity is what makes people feel guilty. Drinking too much or using illegal drugs is taken for granted. Profane and obscene language is not even noticed.

Yet it is not true that people in these circles have no

concern for morality. They often exhibit fantastic moral zeal and passionate, costly moral commitments. They are dedicated to causes. They are involved in politics; they will organize demonstrations. They will sacrifice their money, their time, their comforts, even their freedom for a cause they believe in. Such idealism and involvement is laudable; the problem is, this concern with social morality and indifference to personal morality can result in a moral schizophrenia. I have known of people who refuse to tolerate chemicals in their food who think nothing of injecting chemicals into their bodies. I have known of people who put their bodies through rigorous disciplines of self-denial in the name of physical fitness, but who would not dream of denying their bodies sexual pleasure. I have known of people who are sincerely outraged about the slaughter of baby seals, but who quite ardently support abortion, the slaughter of baby humans.

The tendency today in many academic and professional circles is to see morality in social terms rather than individual terms. In this view, ethics has to do with the behavior of society. Social justice, human rights, concern for the poor, involvement in the political process to make beneficial changes in the social order are at the heart of the moral life. What an individual does is seen as insignificant in light of the major social evils of the day. In fact, an individual's private life, however disordered, may even be seen in terms of a human rights issue that is necessary to protect.

This seems to hold true for conservative circles as well as liberal circles. Whatever the political ideology, right and wrong are seen in terms of the political order. Would we best promote peace by eliminating nuclear weapons or by getting tough with the Russians? Would we help the poor more by increasing welfare or by reducing it? Would we best promote justice by rehabilitating criminals or by executing them? People disagree about ideology and the means to the ends, but both parties tend to agree that world peace, concern for the poor, and social justice are the goals of moral action. At the same time, political conservatives are often just as indifferent to individual morality as political liberals are. Novels by conservative writers will tend to have the same sorts of sexual fantasies and pornographic descriptions as those of their liberal enemies. Right-wing fraternity parties are just as wild and debauched as those of their more liberal classmates, if not more so. For both sides, "voting right" tends to be the ultimate test of moral rectitude.

The Bible, in contrast, teaches that *both* individual morality *and* social morality are important. The books of the prophets are filled with condemnations against the evils of society and demands for social justice (see, for example, Isaiah 58 and Jeremiah 22). Christians must not forget what the Bible says about oppression of the weak and our duty to the poor. Christian ethics does have a social dimension. In this sense, Christians can and should become involved in political and social issues. They can join with their friends and colleagues in being committed to a cause. They will, however, insist upon personal morality as well as social morality. In holding to Biblical absolutes, they will have an advantage even as social reformers.

For some reason people today have the idea that believing in absolute moral standards inhibits social reform. Believing in situational ethics and moral relativism seems somehow more humane and liberal than believing in transcendent absolutes such as the Ten Commandments. The irony is that the view that "what is right for one person isn't necessarily right for someone else" actually undercuts social criticism and beneficial social change. As Chesterton observes, to want to change society presupposes an ideal which we want to work towards. If the ideals are not fixed, then nothing will be changed. "Let beliefs fade fast and frequently, if you wish institutions to remain the same."[1]

By giving transcendent moral principles, the Bible makes social criticism possible. Babylon, like other pagan societies, had no concept of any higher moral authority than the existing social order. The king was not simply a political ruler but a god (see Daniel 6:6-13). In mythological societies the social order, the natural cycles, and the religious realm are all one. To criticize the king, to question the established laws and practices, were, quite literally, unthinkable to the Babylonians. They could not think such thoughts. It was the Bible that introduced into Western civilization the idea of a moral law that transcends the social order. Because these are the laws of God, even kings are subject to them (see Jeremiah 22:1-3). Society itself is to be changed if it violates the higher law. Social criticism and social change of the sort that is taken for granted in the West is unheard of in other cultures. The difference is the profound impact of the Bible, from which even unbelievers cannot escape.[2]

The prevailing view is that Biblical morality is oppressive and that it stands in the way of social change. Nothing is further from the truth. Christianity shut down the bloody games of Rome and put a stop to the time-honored slaughter of the unwanted children. (In rejecting Biblical morality, the present age is bringing back the nightmares of the unenlightened past, as evident in the violence and degradation of our entertainment and the social policy of abortion-on-demand.) The barbarians who conquered Rome were themselves conquered by the Word of God, which dismantled the elaborate codes of revenge and blood feuds which were at the very heart of the Teutonic social system. The aristocratic social structure of the late Middle Ages was smashed by the impact of the Word of God as reemphasized in the Reformation. It was the Bible-believing Christians who abolished the slave trade in England and challenged the worst abuses of industrialism—child labor, the inhuman working conditions, the long hours with subsistence pay.

In the United States, the abolitionist firebrand John Brown and the populist William Jennings Bryan were evangelical Christians. The great social movements of the nineteenth century—abolition, women's suffrage, populism, and, of course, prohibition (which was then closely linked to the other three)—were all animated by Christians who had a high view of Scripture and its impact on society. The civil rights movement was born in the black church with support from Christians all across America. Today Christians are almost alone in standing up for the lives and the rights of those who are being slaughtered in their mother's wombs. Christians have always cared for the poor, the sick, and the oppressed. Despite different methods and ideologies, they have always worked for peace and justice. When Christians become involved in politics, there is always the danger of confusing the Kingdom of God with earthly kingdoms. Mistakes and the unseemly use of power can obscure the gospel, but Christians have always been social activists.

True social morality in fact can only have meaning in the context of individual morality. It has been observed that the Bible does not say, "Love the human race"; instead, it says, "Love your neighbor" (Leviticus 19:18; Matthew 22:39). There is a big difference. It is easier to love humanity in the abstract than to love the very real, concrete individual with whom you have to deal every day. I have known people who are zealots for vast social causes, who are very concerned for the oppressed masses of the world, but who are grossly insensitive and even cruel to the real human beings around them. Conversely, I have known people with the most wrong-headed, insensitive political ideas who are personally warm, generous, and sensitive to people whom they actually come in contact with.

It is very easy to push our moral impulses out to the farthest boundaries of our lives. We can have the "right" views on social and political issues (whatever they might be) and feel quite righteous about it all and morally indignant at those who do not share those views. The Bible, though, is interested in morality in the concrete, not morality in the abstract. It demands not simply that we vote a certain way, but that we live a certain way. It is not enough to support government programs that help the poor; we are told to give to the poor ourselves.

When our consciences are preoccupied with matters on the periphery of our experience, we can often allow ourselves to do pretty much whatever we want. Even worse, we can devise principles to justify whatever we want to do. Promiscuous sex can be justified when it is thought of as sexual expression or sexual freedom. When a man leaves his wife and children to run off with a teenage girl, it can be made to sound almost noble if he thinks of it in terms of his personal growth or personal fulfillment. Modern psychology tends to encourage this sort of language, stressing the fulfillment of the self as the highest goal. When vices are made to sound like virtues, and virtues are made easy for us to satisfy, we begin to cultivate the sin that is more damning than all the rest, the evil that is worse than any sexual perversion and that threatens even Christians: self-righteousness.

THE LAW AND THE GOSPEL

Morality, Christians must admit, is not enough. Christians can agree with other philosophies and world views when it comes to moral issues. The Bible teaches that God's moral law is universal, inscribed in the hearts of human beings and accessible even through natural reason (Romans 2:14-16). In opposing abortion or homosexuality, Christians are not trying to impose their religion on everyone else. Morality has nothing to do with our distinct religious beliefs but agrees with the ethics taught by all religions and, until recently, by all thoughtful secular ideologies. The distinctive belief of Christians is that we are not saved by our moral behavior, since we have little of that to offer to a holy God and are intrinsically sinful. Rather, we are saved by the death and resurrection of Jesus Christ.

Cynicism is fashionable these days. There is a Christian cynicism that we should cultivate. Although we must act in a moral way on both the individual and the social levels, we must remain profoundly skeptical about human beings, about society, and about ourselves. Society and individuals cannot be perfected. People will always sin and institutions will always fail. Christian action will not result in a utopia at which point moral reform can cease. Christian action must always continue in what Chesterton describes as a "perpetual revolution."[3] The sordid politics of a social movement, its degeneration into power struggles and twisted goals need not crush the Christian's ideals. Again, the doctrine of original sin prevents us from becoming disillusioned. We should have no illusions in the first place.

The most dangerous illusion of them all is self-righteousness. This is the true barrier to Jesus Christ. All rejection of God's grace takes this form. Those who refuse the free forgiveness of God through Christ do so because they do not see themselves as needing that forgiveness. They do not admit that they are sinners. They deny that they are desperately lost. God's law in its purity works not only to shape society and to show us how we are to live, but also reveals our sinfulness and awakens in us our need of a Savior (Romans 7; Galatians 3). And yet we try to convince ourselves, even in the midst of our sins, that we are basically good, in fact better than most people. We justify ourselves, and in our complacency and self-sufficient pride we shut out the grace of God.

The self-serving and abstract morality of our modern culture helps to shield us from the horrible, dizzying realization that we are sinners in need of Christ. Evil always presents itself as something good. No one says, "Hey, let's do something evil today." Evil associates itself with a noble cause or with high-sounding words. Abortion associates itself with the emancipation of women. Illicit sex associates itself with love. Cruelty to a friend associates itself with honesty. Selfishness associates itself with integrity and honor. Thus, even manifest sinners cling steadfastly to their own righteousness. A collective, abstract social morality or a legalistic works-righteousness of a religious system can both insulate a person from the truth, salving the conscience and creating the exquisite pleasure of self-righteousness.

The moral absolutes of Scripture, however, are so pure and so corrosive to human pride that they expose our moral failures for what they are: damnable sin against God and against our neighbors. When we realize that we are sinners, that despite all of our best efforts we do not do what we know is right, then the gospel of Jesus Christ, who has borne our sins and who offers up His righteousness, becomes very good news indeed, and the Holy Spirit is unleashed into our lives. Christians confronting modern thought and culture must uphold the law of God against all temptations and pressures. But, avoiding both sin and Pharisaism in their own lives, they must above all uphold the gospel, proclaiming Christ's message of forgiveness and new life to a confused and broken world.

EIGHT

INTELLECTUAL COMBAT

*B*eneath the appearances of academic debate, the genteel discussions over coffee in the faculty lounge, the sophisticated give and take in a classroom discussion, and the publication of learned articles lie matters of life and death. St. Paul shows both the spiritual issues at stake and the tactics that Christians are to use:

> For though we live in the world we are not carrying on a worldly war, for the weapons of our warfare are not worldly but have divine power to destroy strongholds. We destroy arguments and every proud obstacle to the knowledge of God, and take every thought captive to obey Christ. (2 Corinthians 10:3-5)

Christians engaged in modern thought and culture are indeed "in the world." The war they are involved in, though, is more than worldly. The existence of God, the nature of moral values, the historicity of the Bible—all of these issues are more than interesting controversies or intellectually stimulating exercises. How one resolves these questions can help determine the destiny of one's immortal soul. In the classroom, in the dormitory, in the faculty lounge, wherever such things are discussed, souls can be destroyed or saved.

WEAPONS

Christians engaged in such discussions can be confident. Just as the intellectual combat is at heart a spiritual one, their weapons are not merely intellectual but spiritual as well. "The weapons of our warfare are not worldly but have divine power to destroy strongholds." These weapons are God's law, which brings conviction of sin, and the gospel of Jesus Christ, which can penetrate the hardest of hearts to bring life and to create faith.

In other words, the Christian's weapon is "the sword of the Spirit, which is the word of God" (Ephesians 6:17). God's Word is the means whereby the Holy Spirit operates on the hearts and minds of its hearers. When a person reads the Bible or hears its truths in a sermon, a personal discussion, or even an academic article, the Holy Spirit is at work in a powerful way, destroying the strongholds of rationalization and sin which human beings erect to shut out God.

A person grounded in Scripture and explaining its message has "divine power." A college freshman stuttering out the doctrine of the Incarnation in an Ivy League philosophy class may lose the verbal swordplay against a sophisticated and quick-witted professor. But the effectiveness of the testimony does not depend upon the skill of its presentation, only upon the Holy Spirit who is at work in that testimony.

This was true even with St. Paul, who said that he was not eloquent, nor did he use "plausible words" in proclaiming the "foolishness" of the gospel, "that your faith might not rest in the wisdom of men but in the power of God" (1 Corinthians 2:5). A Christian student, however buffeted by opposing arguments, can have the confidence of the Psalmist: "I have more understanding than all my teachers, for thy testimonies are my meditation" (Psalm 119:99). A Christian teacher or writer can have the confidence that God's Word will not return to Him empty, but will accomplish His purposes (Isaiah 55:11).

DESTROYING STRONGHOLDS

It is significant that St. Paul's method of argument described in the passage from 2 Corinthians 10 is essentially negative. He is not so concerned with arguing positively for the truths of the faith—he leaves that to the efficacy of the Word. Rather, he destroys arguments and casts down obstacles that people erect against the knowledge of God. Apologetics can be useful in presenting Christianity. We have been told to "always be prepared to make a defense to any one who calls you to account for the hope that is in you" (1 Peter 3:15). Still, the combat as St. Paul describes it here is not defensive but offensive. It is a matter of challenging and refuting the proud arguments behind which sinners hide from their God.

This negative method is especially suited for the Christian in academia. One may not be able to prove the existence of God to a skeptic's satisfaction, but one can examine the skeptic's philosophy and reveal its limitations and errors. ("Do you really believe that life is chaotic and meaningless? Where is the chaos in biology, for instance? Perhaps you mean emotional or moral chaos. . . .") It may be difficult to argue the case for scientific creationism in a convincing way to secular scientists. It is much easier to bring out some very real difficulties in Darwin's theory of evolution which secular scientists themselves are finding.[1]

All of the secular teachings which oppose themselves to Christianity—Marxism, existentialism, materialism, humanism, not to mention the pop theologies and pop psychologies of the best-seller lists—are all vulnerable to critical analysis. It is not always necessary to attack them from an explicitly religious perspective. It may be more effective if religion is left out of it. One can simply unveil the logical contradictions, the contrary evidence, the manifest silliness that these views will usually involve.

The goal is to "destroy arguments," to cast down "proud obstacles," to demolish "strongholds." To do so, the Christian may employ the methods of critical analysis taught as a major part of the modern intellectual enterprise. Christians engaged in the intellectual warfare will often feel beleaguered and defensive. It is much more fun to be on the offensive.

TAKING EVERY THOUGHT CAPTIVE

In addition to "destroying arguments," St. Paul urges us to "take every thought captive to obey Christ." His military metaphor, calling to mind the Israelites' warfare against the

Canaanites, pictures an assault on a walled stronghold. The walls are torn down and "every thought" is captured and made to submit to Christ the King. Here Scripture brings all intellectual activity under the Lordship of Christ. "Every thought"—that includes everything from mathematical abstractions to the fantasies of the imagination—is claimed by Jesus Christ.

To be sure, fugitives are often hard to capture. They run and hide, and when cornered they fight. The process of capturing thoughts is described in terms of violent struggle. Yet this Scripture clearly implies that every thought *can* obey Christ. Every idea, every fact, every discovery can be changed from a "proud obstacle" to an obedient servant. This is Christ's desire, and He equips with "divine power" those whom He has called to this combat.

The passage from 2 Corinthians embraces both functions of the intellectual process. "Destroying arguments" corresponds to the progressive impulse, the need to question, criticize, and change. "Taking every thought captive" reflects the traditionalist impulse. Captives must be guarded and held. Obedience to Christ is held up as the absolute principle. Traditionalism guards and preserves thoughts once captured.

Scripture thus opens up the whole realm of the intellectual life to Christians. Like Canaan and like Babylon, this realm is usually hostile territory. Daniel, though, was a bearer of God's Word. This Word gave him stability. He carried it to the academy and to the courts of the world empire. This Word eventually brought judgment, conviction, and even, the Scripture implies, conversion to Nebuchadnezzar himself (Daniel 4:34-37).

Christians will often feel like the Israelites besieged by the Babylonian hosts, assailed on all sides, defeated, humiliated. Christians can also be like Joshua and the army of Israel, razing the walls of Jericho through the power of the Word of God. What Christians must not do is shrink from the combat, refusing to think or to confront opposing ideas. To do so is to leave the field to the enemy and to deny Christ the full extent of His reign.

PART THREE

THE CHRISTIAN MIND

NINE

THE COMMUNION OF THE SAINTS

*H*aving explored some of the intellectual and moral dis-agreements between Christianity and modern thought, we can turn from the negative to the positive. The Christian life and the Biblical world view can not only withstand critical inquiry, but they can inspire critical inquiry. Christianity is a positive advantage to the person who seeks knowledge and truth. Daniel, Shadrach, Meshach, and Abednego proved themselves "ten times better than all the magicians and en-chanters" at the University of Babylon (Daniel 1:21). Not only were Daniel and the others allowed to study at Babylon, but they excelled. Modern Christians may not be able to attain the same ratio over their unbelieving colleagues, but the principle seems to be that those faithful to the God of the Bible have an actual advantage in the pursuit of knowledge.

The intellectual resources of Christianity are vast and rich. Christians, though, must learn to draw on those re-sources; if they do not, it will be difficult for them to stand against the onslaughts of the unbelieving mind.

One of the Christian's most precious, and often most underused, resources is the Church. The Bible teaches that a group of Christians becomes greater than the sum of its parts. "For where two or three are gathered in my name, there am I in the midst of them" (Matthew 18:20). When even two Christians come together in the name of Christ, Jesus Him-self is there. In fact, groups of ordinary Christians make up no less than the Body of Christ (1 Corinthians 12:12-27).

It is difficult to be a Christian by oneself, especially in a hostile environment. Christ ordained that the Christian is to be nourished and supported by other Christians. The local church, fellowship with other believers in one's profession or field, the solidarity with the Christian Church through the ages, with its store of wisdom and with its great intellectual tradition—all of these manifestations of the universal Church can be a bulwark against the intellectual and moral temptations of the modern age. The Church can also offer support, direction, inspiration, and a rich, complex source of ideas that can provide a context and a foundation for one's own studies. Christian students and thinkers need to take advantage of the spiritual and intellectual interplay that can be found in what the creeds refer to as "the communion of the saints."

WORLDLINESS

Being a part of the community that is the Church is extremely helpful in battling what may be the most subtle and damaging temptation of them all in academic, professional, or intellectual circles: worldliness. The desire to be accepted by colleagues, to be fashionable, to fit in with the dominant social or intellectual circle, is very powerful. Such desires may be innocent at first, but after a while they can make the Christian faith seem embarrassing, then an obstacle to full acceptance by the group. The desire to be intellectually respectable can lead to hybrid breeds of secularism and Christianity as seen in modern liberal theology or to sheer unbelief. The desire to be socially respectable can erode the sternness of Biblical morality into a free and easy tolerance that can come to excuse, both in others and in oneself, the rankest immorality.

Such peer pressure (which is just as common in adults as in young people, by the way) is what the Bible means when it warns against the temptations of "the world." The Church can offer a counterweight, a good peer pressure, so to speak, that can keep a person from sliding away into conformity with an unbelieving world. Such conformity not only can be caustic to faith, but it is also stifling intellectually.

One form of peer pressure common in academia and other professions is that of social class. Peter Berger, the great contemporary sociologist, argues that there is a new elite in American society, a social class that is based not upon wealth, as in the old social classes, but upon information and the manipulation of symbols and knowledge. This new elite social class includes educators, journalists, artists, members of the helping professions, social scientists, and government workers. This new class tends to stress liberal social, intellectual, and moral values. It is thus in conflict with the old business class, with its more conservative, business-oriented values. Because academics and intellectuals find themselves in this particular social class, they will experience pressure to conform to its beliefs and symbols.

Berger points out, for example, how difficult it is for a faculty member in a typical modern university to admit having conservative values. Friends, colleagues, and the academic institutions themselves exert pressure upon the faculty member to exhibit the class values of moral libertarianism and progressive social theories. Such acculturation is casual and informal, but the small talk in the faculty lounge, the jokes, and the social atmosphere tend to enforce an ideology. Certain opinions and attitudes become symbols of right thinking, of solidarity with the world of intellectuals and scholars. As Berger points out,

> The symbols of class culture are important. They allow people to "sniff out" who belongs and who does not; they provide easily applied criteria of "soundness." Thus a young instructor applying for a job in an elite university is well advised to hide "unsound" views such as political allegiance to the right wing of the Republican party (perhaps even to the left wing), opposition to abortion or to other causes of the feminist movement, or a strong commitment to the virtues of the corporation.[1]

Believing in abortion has thus become a shibboleth for the new elite. The young instructor may never get a job at that elite university if such "unsound" views are detected. If the instructor does get the job, in a few years of acculturation in the faculty club, those "conservative" views may very well give way to ones that are more socially acceptable. The same pattern is no doubt behind the political phenomenon of conservative officeholders becoming more liberal to the extent that they become involved in the social life of Washington, D.C.

This class struggle, as Berger describes it, is also manifested in the contemporary Church. The mainline theological establishment—theologians at prestigious universities, Church leaders who manage large bureaucracies, and ministers grounded in the social sciences or helping professions—is also part of the "new class." Berger goes even further:

> One of the easiest empirical procedures to determine very quickly what the agenda of the new class is at any given moment is to look up the latest pronouncements of the National Council of Churches and, to a somewhat lesser extent, of the denominational organizations of mainline Protestantism.[2]

Berger does believe, at the same time, that "the Christian New Right represents the agenda of the business class (and of other strata interested in material production) with which the new class is locked in religious battle."[3]

It is probably inevitable and, to a certain extent, theologically indifferent for political beliefs to be shaped by social class, special interests, and other secular concerns. The moral and religious beliefs of a Christian, on the other hand, need to be shaped by the Word of God, not by the world. Christians need to be critical thinkers and to use discernment, forging their own ideology based on Scripture, not the social class that they aspire to. Christians should not be so easily labeled. "Thus," says Berger, "one might conclude on grounds of Christian ethics that the new class is 'more Christian' in its resolute antagonism to racism, but 'less Christian' in its uncritical allegiance to the cause of abortion."[4]

The point is, social pressures can and do erode Christian orthodoxy, probably more than any actual intellectual arguments. Ironically and tragically, the temptations of the world increase in direct proportion to one's success. When a Christian starts to succeed—academically, financially, politically, or professionally—the world will become more and more seductive. With prestige comes dependence upon the opinion of others. With status comes the invitation to join the "inner circles."[5] With the feeding of one's pride comes self-deification. I do believe Christians can be successful, but they must beware of what temptations they will face. They will also need the ministry of the Church.

DANIEL AND CHRISTIAN FELLOWSHIP

When Daniel was in Babylon, he relied on the support of his fellow-believers. Four Hebrews bound together in fellowship and prayer were able to withstand the temptation of conforming to the status and glory of Imperial Babylon. Daniel's experience as described in Scripture gives a model for how a Christian in a hostile environment can draw on the spiritual strength of other believers.

After Daniel's formal education was completed, the whole academic community of which Daniel had become a part was almost put to the sword. It began when Nebuchadnezzar had a bad dream. The king had the feeling that the dream was important, but, as with most dreams, he could not even remember what it was. He summoned the academic community and insisted that they tell him what his dream was and what it meant. "Tell us what the dream was," they replied, "and we will interpret it." The king would not make it so easy:

> The king answered the Chaldeans, "The word from me is sure: if you do not make known to me the dream and its interpretation, you shall be torn limb from limb, and your houses shall be laid in ruins." . . . The Chaldeans answered the king, "There is not a man on earth who can meet the king's demand; for no great and powerful king has

> asked such a thing of any magician or enchanter or
> Chaldean. The thing that the king asks is difficult,
> and none can show it to the king except the gods,
> whose dwelling is not with flesh." Because of this
> the king was angry and very furious, and command-
> ed that all the wise men of Babylon be destroyed.
> (Daniel 2:5, 10-12)

Nebuchadnezzar was asking for the impossible. His "wise
men," however insightful they might be, could not read his
mind. Nebuchadnezzar exploded. "What am I paying you
people for if you cannot answer a simple question that is
tormenting me?"

Even today people are infuriated when intellectuals cannot answer questions that are impossible for them to answer:
How can we decrease crime? Why are our children misbehav-
ing? When does life begin? What should we do about genetic
engineering or the threat of nuclear war? How can we establish the perfect society? Such questions of values and the
mysteries of the human condition ever elude confident answers from human wisdom, and we become frustrated when
our great "thinkers" are, as they must be, as mystified by all
of this as anyone else.

The result of Nebuchadnezzar's frustration was the
threat of an anti-intellectual bloodbath. In the Red Guard
frenzy in China, scholars and teachers were routinely round-
ed up and brutalized simply for being intellectuals. The
Khmer Rouge in Cambodia at one point killed anyone with
glasses because that was evidence that the person could read.
The same sort of violent anti-intellectualism breaks out from
time to time. Christians are usually also victims in these
crusades against anyone who thinks.

> So the decree went forth that the wise men were to
> be slain, and they sought Daniel and his compan-
> ions, to slay them. Then Daniel replied with pru-
> dence and discretion to Arioch, the captain of the
> king's guard, who had gone out to slay the wise men
> of Babylon; he said to Arioch, the king's captain,

"Why is the decree of the king so severe?" Then
Arioch made the matter known to Daniel. And
Daniel went in and besought the king to appoint
him a time, that he might show to the king the
interpretation. (Daniel 2:13-16)

Daniel was one of the "wise men" condemned to be slaughtered. He replied with courtesy and respect even to his execu-
tioner, another striking example of his submission to authority. This bought him some time. Daniel made the appoint-
ment with the king before he had any idea what the dream
was about or what he would say. He acted in faith.

Immediately, he went to his fellow-believers:

Then Daniel went to his house and made the matter
known to Hananiah, Mishael, and Azariah, his companions, and told them to seek mercy of the God of
heaven concerning this mystery, so that Daniel and
his companions might not perish with the rest of
the wise men of Babylon. Then the mystery was
revealed to Daniel in a vision of the night. (Daniel
2:17-19)

Daniel prayed, a valuable weapon in the believer's arsenal. He
did not just pray by himself, though. He asked his three
friends to pray for him. He "told *them* to seek mercy of the
God of heaven concerning this mystery." Certainly God answers solitary prayer, but there seems to be special power in
the prayer of a group. "If two of you agree on earth about
anything they ask, it will be done for them by my Father in
heaven" (Matthew 18:19). At any rate, Daniel himself felt a
need for the support of the group. Immediately after he was
confronted with this insoluble problem, he sought out "his
companions" in the faith.

That night God gave Daniel exactly what he needed to
know. This crisis led to Daniel's great prophecy of Christ
triumphing over the world kingdoms (Daniel 2). The outcome was an opportunity to witness for the true God that
made Nebuchadnezzar himself acknowledge the God of Israel

(2:47). What looked to be disaster led to the advancement of God's people as Daniel was made ruler over all of the pagan wise men and his companions were made rulers in Babylon.

The principle here seems to be that Christians in a hostile environment need to seek out other Christians in that hostile environment to support each other in fellowship and prayer. Bible studies, prayer groups, and Christian friendships can be spiritual anchors. On a college campus, that might mean getting involved with organized campus ministries or informal Bible study groups or simply getting to know other Christians in one's dorm or classes. At work that might mean finding out about other Christians in the company or in one's profession.

To meet together with other Christians for Bible study and prayer is to tap enormous spiritual power. This will seem especially true when confronting hostility to the faith. Encountering spiritual opposition can make a Christian hunger for God's Word, drawing from it nourishment that is constantly renewing and life-giving. When a person is engaged in spiritual combat, the Bible seems to speak most clearly and most intimately. A text will sometimes almost leap up out of the page. My college Bible is marked to tatters by underlining, notes, and dates referring to situations and problems that were directly spoken to in my daily Bible reading and in the insights of my friends as we studied the Scriptures.

Praying with and for other Christians is also a vast spiritual resource. Few of us realize how powerful prayer is. To share one's needs and to accept the prayers of others is to experience true spiritual intimacy. Conversely, to take not simply one's own needs but those of another person before God in prayer is to experience selflessness and true love for another person. God answers those prayers and in so doing builds up the solidarity of His Body, the Church.

It is a mysterious fact of history that the Church is always at its best when it encounters the most opposition. When the Roman Empire was slaughtering Christians by the thousands, the Church seemed most real, most pure. The Age of the Martyrs is always the Golden Age of the Church. During the Reformation, people were given the choice of either renouncing the gospel or being burned alive. On the mission field, many missionaries have been killed because of their message. In many places, to be baptized means a death sentence. Today, in the Soviet Union, Eastern Europe, China, and other places of religious oppression, the Christians who meet together secretly, treasuring worn fragments of the Bible and risking their very lives to worship Christ, are heroes of the faith. Whenever the Church encounters persecution, the true power of the Holy Spirit is made manifest.

The opposition is not so severe on modern campuses or professional circles. Still, the hostility of the modern intellectual establishment to orthodox Christianity can and does create Christian fellowship that is purer and more alive than one often finds in less dangerous environments. There are few who are Christians in name only in campus fellowship groups. Those who band together in the face of opposition are highly committed to their cause. Nominal Christians and the uncommitted will not bother. As a result, the Christian fellowship one experiences in college, for example, tends to be unusually vital, rich, and inspiring.

College Christians often experience a crisis when they graduate and move away from the campus. They become used to an intense kind of fellowship, Bible study, and mutual support that is difficult to find in an ordinary church. The point is, the Church thrives in a hostile atmosphere, not only in spite of the opposition it encounters, but because of the opposition.

THE LOCAL CHURCH

Informal fellowship as experienced in Christian friendships, Bible studies, and prayer groups is no substitute, however, for the local church. Modern-day Christians often prefer to meet with people just like themselves in informal settings, disdaining the institutional Church. This can be a dangerous mistake. The best safeguard against elitism, which is the sure mark of worldliness, is intense involvement in the local church. Most churches contain people with whom we would never associate on our own. Yet in the Church, something wonderful and profound takes place. People from every age-group, every occupation and social class, will all come together on Sunday morning to unite in worship of their Lord: the wealthy banker, the farmer, the elderly widow, the four-year-old; the well-educated, the illiterate; the highly sophisticated, the naive and uncultured. In the Church the infinite variety of human beings—all ages, occupations, interests, and personalities—are united in Jesus Christ.

It is natural and desirable to associate with people with whom we have things in common, to form homogenous groups based on age, interests, social background, or academic field. This can have its value, as long as relationships with the rich texture of humanity are not neglected. The "ordinary" people of one's local parish ought never be despised.

Christianity calls into existence a diverse community of believers. The Christian ethic is based on love, and love implies relationships. Although it may be easier to love if we never have to actually deal with anyone, Biblical love is that messy kind that means getting involved with real people. This requires people meeting together and sharing their lives and faith with people who are as different from each other as a foot is from an eye (1 Corinthians 12:14-26). The problem with private Bible study groups alone is that they can tend to be made up of all feet or all eyes.

The ordinary church on the corner, if it holds to Scripture and proclaims Christ, has been established by God for the sake of His Kingdom. Worship of the living God is to be done not only individually but corporately, as the whole body of believers in all of their diversity comes together to hear the Word of God proclaimed and to sing praises to God. In corporate worship Christians also take part in the Christ-ordained rites of baptism and Holy Communion, in which our union with Christ and with each other is made manifest most intimately. Christians, no matter how intellectually sophisticated they might be, should submit to the discipline and the fellowship of a local congregation, and in doing so they will find a precious spiritual resource.

THE UNIVERSAL CHURCH

The Body of Christ includes not only one's Christian friends and local church. It includes all believers in Christ around the world. It extends also back through time to include the believers in Christ who lived and died hundreds of years ago. Someone who believes in Jesus Christ is unified with all other Christians, living and dead. As organic members of Christ's Body, we become part of the company of all the saints. Paul of Tarsus, Augustine, Francis of Assisi, John Hus, Martin Luther, John Wesley, William Wilberforce, Mother Teresa, Billy Graham, the Christians in the Soviet prison camps—all of these Christians, in all of their variety, partake of the same Holy Spirit who has drawn us also into the Christian faith. This universal Church, with its rich intellectual tradition and its heritage of spiritual wisdom and example, is a strong ally for someone trying to take on the modern secular establishment.

According to the Bible, each individual believer is made part of the entire company of saints:

> So then you are no longer strangers and sojourners, but you are fellow citizens with the saints and members of the household of God, built upon the foundation of the apostles and prophets, Christ Jesus himself being the cornerstone, in whom the whole structure is joined together and grows into a holy temple in the Lord; in whom you also are built into it for a dwelling place of God in the Spirit. (Ephesians 2:19-22)

> For just as the body is one and has many members, and all the members of the body, though many, are one body, so it is with Christ. For by one Spirit we were all baptized into one body—Jews or Greeks, slaves or free—and all were made to drink of one Spirit. . . . If one member suffers, all suffer together; if one member is honored, all rejoice together. (1 Corinthians 12:12, 13, 26)

There is certainly variety in the universal Church—different personalities, different cultures, different traditions. Biblical unity is not drab uniformity, neither the nothingness of Eastern religions which eradicate individuality and uniqueness, nor a bureaucratic lowest common denominator. Instead, the

Bible stresses a unity of things that are very different from each other. This unity amidst diversity is imaged in the human body. The lungs are nothing like a toe, the spleen is not even close to an eyeball, but all of these individual organs nevertheless work together and make up one body.

The same is true in the Church. The usher standing in the back of the sanctuary passing out bulletins may not seem very similar to Justin Martyr who was killed for his faith in the second century, but those differences should not obscure the very real unity they have in Jesus Christ. Even in the discords and theological disagreements which mar the outward unity of the church, there is a fundamental oneness among true believers in Christ.[6]

The Christians of the past constitute a heritage of spirituality and insight which can be especially helpful for present-day Christians in academia. Through God's great gift of writing, ideas can be stored and passed on to other generations. Even after an individual dies, his or her mind and insights can live on, preserved forever in the pages of a book. When we read, we can tap in to a great Christian's mind, sharing in the person's faith, experience, and wisdom. Reading the works of Christians through the ages—Augustine and Eusebius, Aquinas and Dante, Luther and Calvin, Herbert and Milton, Wesley and Johnson, MacDonald and Chesterton, Eliot and Lewis—is similar to the commerce of minds and faith that one finds in an unusually lively Bible study. The same kind of nourishment, the same kind of "communion of the saints," is possible, working not only vertically through people in our own circles, but horizontally through time.

Modern-day Christians are heirs to a great Christian intellectual tradition. This tradition of active thought and practical problem-solving is a vital ally for Christians fighting against the intellectual trends of the modern world. Drawing on the insights of the past can give a valuable perspective on present-day issues. We can thus be freed from the tyranny of the present, the assumption that the way people think today is the only possible way to think.[7]

If confused by modern atheistic and nihilistic philosophy, read some classic Christian philosophers. By any criterion, who is the better philosopher, Nietzsche or St. Thomas Aquinas? If troubled with modern theologians who deny the truths of Scripture, take a look at the Church Fathers, the theologians of the first few centuries after Christ. Notice along with C. S. Lewis how the "new" theologies turn out to be simply old, worn-out heresies that real theologians dismissed a long time ago.[8]

If interested in the arts and literature, but disturbed because your artistic friends despise your faith, saturate yourself in Bach, Rembrandt, and Milton. Or, if you need someone more modern, study Poulenc, Roualt, and T. S. Eliot. How do these Christian artists measure up? Aren't they rather impressive, even to your nonbelieving friends?

If you are interested in science, but having difficulties reconciling science to Scripture, read almost any of the founders of modern science, who were also usually devout Christians. Read Sir Isaac Newton. Or, for a real jolt of spiritual energy, read Blaise Pascal. Notice how religious faith and scientific knowledge can actually build on each other.

Whatever your field of study or interest, do some extra research and find the Christians who were also involved in that field. There are almost always some; often they are the pioneers, the intellectual giants of the discipline.

In addition to the thinkers of the past, make contact with the Christian thinkers of the present. For a time it seemed that Bible-believing Protestants had abandoned the battleground, leaving the academic debate and the great questions of the modern world to the secularists. That is the case no longer.

When I was in college, I remember looking for a Christian response to existentialism and other ideas I was confronted with in college. The best resource I could find was *The Catholic Encyclopedia*. It was genuinely helpful. Catholicism's rich intellectual tradition has kept abreast of modernist ideas and subjected them to a Christian critique. As a Protestant, I wished my fellow-Protestants would do more. Later I discovered the world of evangelical scholarship, which is continually growing more vigorous and more sophisticated. Subscribing to *Christianity Today* helped put me in touch with this kind of thinking. I also started hanging out at a good Christian bookstore. I found writers such as Francis Schaeffer taking on the whole Western tradition from the point of view of Biblical Christianity. I discovered theologians such as Carl Henry, who magisterially answered my questions about philosophy and modern theologians. I was already familiar with C. S. Lewis, that most indispensable of modern Christian writers, but I found author after author, book after book, that dealt in a Biblical way with topics and issues I was facing in academia.

I discovered whole publishing companies devoted to exploring the relationship between the Christian faith and every area of life—Crossway, InterVarsity Press, Baker, Zondervan, Eerdmans, etc., etc. There are also scholarly journals that relate one's subject specialty to the Christian faith. *Christian Scholar's Review* offers a broad-ranging sampling of Christian scholarship with reviews that can alert one to the latest books on nearly every topic. In my field there is *Christianity and Literature*, and similar specialized Christian periodicals exist for almost every profession and field of study. There are also organizations in which Christians of the same profession— scientists, nurses, attorneys, business executives—can make contact with each other for mutual fellowship and support.

Today it is possible to find the Christian point of view on nearly every topic of debate, in nearly every field of knowledge. The social sciences and the hard sciences, the humanities and the vocations have all been sensitively explored by Christian writers. Subjects such as clinical psychology, creationism vs. evolution, the dynamics of the arts, the foundations of political action, the ethical problems in the fields of nursing or business have all been treated in a helpful way by people applying the Word of God to modern thought and experience.

A special manifestation of the Church engaged in the pursuit of knowledge is the Christian school and the Christian college. Here Christian faculty and Christian students can join together in a fellowship that is both intellectual and spiritual. Here the integration of Christianity with all areas of knowledge and of life is the daily work and the basic assumption of the whole institution. Here Christian scholarship and Christian thinking is encouraged and nourished. Strong, excellent Christian colleges are an important arm of the Church as a whole.

There is still a great deal to do. The Christian intellectual tradition needs to be passed on to new generations of thinkers. It needs to be reinvigorated. There are still many questions that have not yet been fully answered. There are errors that need to be challenged and truths that need to be defended. The Christian community needs the support of Christian thinkers, and secular thought needs persuasive, effective applications of Biblical truths.

The individual Christian can find nourishment and support in the Church. In a hostile climate, the company of fellow-believers is essential. Christians today may draw on and become a part of the Christian intellectual tradition that has had such an impact on the world. One of the keys in resolving the dilemmas that a Christian will face in the modern world is to realize that no Christian need face any problem alone.

TEN

THE MAGICIANS AND THE ENCHANTERS

At the end of the account of Daniel and friends' three years at the University of Babylon, the Bible concludes with a verse that is very important for a Biblical view of education: "As for these four youths, God gave them learning and skill in all letters and wisdom" (Daniel 1:17). God gave them learning, as He had already given them the skill. The Bible here clearly states that God is the source of knowledge, even so-called secular or pagan knowledge. "*All* letters and wisdom" come under the sovereignty of God and are described here as His gift.

At the end of their three-year program, Daniel, Shadrach, Meschach, and Abdednego had, in effect, a final exam. They were brought in before the king himself and interrogated about what they knew.

At the end of the time, when the king had commanded that they should be brought in, the chief of the eunuchs brought them in before Nebuchadnezzar. And the king spoke with them, and among them all none was found like Daniel, Hananiah, Mishael, and Azariah; therefore they stood before the king. And in every matter of wisdom and understanding concerning which the king inquired of them, he found them ten times better than all the magicians and enchanters that were in all his kingdom. (Daniel 1:18-20)

This oral examination was comprehensive. "In *every* matter of wisdom and understanding" the four believers who would not defile themselves proved to be "ten times better" than their pagan colleagues.

Why was this? The four had been initiated into the sophisticated intellectual climate of Babylon. They also, however, were saturated with the truth of God's Word. The "magicians and enchanters" did not have this extra advantage.

The Babylonian intelligentsia were brilliant, yet limited. They were great engineers and mathematicians. They made great discoveries in astronomy and the other sciences. They created great art and had a rich literature. Their erroneous world views and their pagan superstitions, however, were a real obstacle in their pursuit of truth.

They could predict an eclipse of the moon—think of the sophisticated observations and complex mathematics that involves, all without the aid of telescopes or computers. They worked out this truth with great accuracy and insight. Yet, although their calculations were true, the truth which they discovered was also distorted and partial. They saw the moon and the sun in terms of gods and goddesses. They believed the stars determined human fate. The eclipse which they predicted with such perfect accuracy they also believed was a portent of doom.

Daniel and the others could and did learn the Babylonians' mathematics and other insights. They were not, however, bound by the Babylonians' superstitions or limited by their narrow visions. They learned to predict a lunar eclipse without taking it so seriously. By the same token, contemporary Christians can appropriate the learning of our secular culture without being taken in by its superstitions and narrow visions.

In fact, I would like to hazard a comparison between the intellectual elite of ancient Babylon and the intellectual elite of our own day. The Bible describes the "wise men" of Nebuchadnezzar's court as "magicians and enchanters." The modern world view also tends to see knowledge in terms of what is, in effect, magic and enchantment. Despite the risk of overstating and straining the analogy, exploring the parallels may help us see the peculiar limitations of modern thought, and why Christians can aspire to be "ten times better" than the magicians and enchanters.

THE MAGICIANS

The Babylonian magicians learned to manipulate physical objects to create impressive effects and illusions that dazzled and mystified their audience. Today many scientists are similarly interested only in technological mastery over nature. They develop complicated techniques of controlling nature and making it do their bidding. What they achieve is certainly dazzling, awakening superstitious wonder in those who are not scientists and who come to believe that science alone can solve all human problems. Daniel and modern Christians know, unlike the Babylonian magicians and many contemporary scientists, that there is more to truth than technique and mastery.

The Babylonian magicians also believed that nature is divine. The sun, the moon, the earth, the sky, as well as all of the processes necessary to life—raising crops, having children, obeying rules—are identical with the persons and the activities of the gods. We have already noted how this sacred, mythological view of nature inhibited the development of modern science and how it was the impact of the Bible that desacralized nature and thus opened up the world to objective human inquiry.

Yet today the Babylonian view that nature is divine has returned. Many scientists believe that the physical world is all that exists and is all that has ever existed. They believe, in other words, that nature is eternal. They believe that nature is complete in itself, that it is self-sufficient. They believe that everything that exists—from atoms to planets, from the species of animals to human civilizations—has been called into being by the processes of nature. They even determine moral values according to what is natural.

To speak of something as being eternal and self-sufficient, the source of existence and values, is, of course, to set forth a definition of God. For Christians, it is "the God of

Abraham and Isaac," the Triune, personal God set forth in Scripture, who is eternal, self-sufficient, and the source of existence and values. For many people today, it is the physical world described by the scientific method that is understood as eternal, self-sufficient, and the source of existence and values—in other words, nature takes on all the attributes of God. We see this already in the rapt emotion and the religious language of Carl Sagan. ("The Cosmos is all there is, all there was, and all there ever will be"—the One who is, who was, and is to come, world without end, Amen.) If the physical world is the only ultimate reality, if nature alone is the ground of our being, if there is no transcendent Creator and giver of meaning, then we are, in effect, back to the primitive nature religions.

The process is not complete—the Biblical secularization of nature is still with us. But if Nature takes the place of the God of Abraham, Isaac, and Jacob, science itself, history suggests, may be one of the first casualties. The environmental movement, by and large, is a laudable attempt to control humanity's "magical" exploitation of nature. Yet, I notice the religious overtones of many environmentalists, the idea that nature is sacred and that therefore research of various kinds must be stopped lest we violate something in nature. This is a reemergence of the old taboo way of thinking, which is extremely common in mythological societies and which prevented scientific investigation of nature for centuries. Similar investing of nature with religious powers such as healing and salvation is evident in the health food movement. Whatever is ultimate will be understood as sacred, and what is sacred will be hedged with restrictions, rituals, and warnings against blasphemy. Those who worship nature, paradoxically, tend to resist its being studied.

If nature worship tends ultimately to be antiknowledge, its other casualties, such as human freedom and moral ideals, are more immediate and easier to see. Since the view that nature is absolute became the dominant orthodoxy in Western thought, we have seen a number of societies organized on this principle.

Marxism rests on a rigorous assumption of dialectical

materialism, in which the processes of history, seen as the unfolding of natural evolutionary struggles, are understood as the source of all ideology and policy. Ultimately, for human beings, the society becomes the source of values and the determiner of human fate—again, another god. In postrevolutionary societies, the state becomes divine, just as Babylon—its land, its king, and its laws—was held to be, literally, divine. What that has meant in the Soviet Union is clear: political oppression, violations of individual rights, militarism, suppression of independent scientific inquiry (except for weapons technology and other research to the service of the state), censorship of the arts. There can be no freedom in nature, nor in naturalistic societies. Concepts such as individualism and human rights do not have meaning when there are no objective values that transcend the state, the society, and nature itself.

Fascism is an especially dramatic example of modern neo-paganism. Bolstered by the theories of racial biologists, whose absurd and brutal ideas were considered quite respectable and scientific at the time, fascism developed a cult of "the Land," "the People," and "the Nation" that grew, as paganism easily will if given a chance, into religious frenzy. Hitler invoked the old Germanic gods of war; Mussolini invoked the spirits of pagan Rome. These gods came back. Even sophisticates such as Ezra Pound, the godfather of modernist literature, and Martin Heidegger, the great systematizer of modern existentialism, were caught up in this surge of primitive and specifically demonic feeling. So were many liberal theologians (some of those who had developed scientific criticism of the Bible did so to cast doubt on the Old Testament because it was Jewish).[1] This backlash against Biblical thinking and this unabashed revival of paganism directed itself specifically against the people of the Bible, culminating in the blasphemy of the Holocaust.

Modern democracies too must beware of the neo-pagan climate. If the physical world is the only reality and there are no transcendent moral realities, then decisions will be made solely on the basis of efficiency or what works. Plans and policies will be made in a moral vacuum. Survival of the fittest, a dogma of the evolutionists, becomes a dogma of economists. Without a moral consensus, ideology becomes simply a matter of competing interest groups.

Even a free society can be oppressive and cruel. The Babylonians thought nothing of exposing a baby that they did not want. Abortion is not a new discovery of modern technology, but was practiced extensively in the ancient world.[2] In mythological cultures, a child is valued only insofar as it contributes to the well-being of the family and the community. It has no intrinsic value or individual rights. A few years ago, abortion was unthinkable in Western culture. Today it is very difficult for people to see anything wrong with it. Eventually, what we take for granted now as intrinsic values and individual rights may become literally unthinkable. That is, they may become absolutely foreign concepts to minds that have become totally reoriented and molded to pagan structures of thinking.

THE ENCHANTERS

If the Babylonian magicians are analagous in their mastery of technique and veneration of nature to the modern scientific mentality, the other group which Daniel was superior to, the "enchanters," may be analagous to another major academic world view of modern times. If the magicians correspond to the sciences, the enchanters correspond to the humanities. If the world view of the magicians is related to modern naturalism, the world view of the enchanters may be related to modern humanism.

The enchanter casts a spell over an audience by the power of his words or gestures. He can manipulate people and events at will. He creates illusions or even realities. The enchanter is the creator and manipulator of meaning. The figure of the enchanter makes me think of two figures that exert a powerful hold on the thinking of modern academia: the philosopher and the artist.

Modern philosophy is dominated by a school of thought known as existentialism. Whereas many philosophies and religions have posed answers to the question, "What is the meaning of life?" existentialism solves the problem in a bold way: There is no meaning in life. According to existentialism, life is meaningless, pointless, absurd. There is pattern and order in nature, but it means nothing. There is no purpose. There are no external values. Nothing.

Existentialism is not totally despairing, however. Meaning is possible. A human being will not find a ready-made meaning, but can create personal meaning. Human beings, cast adrift in this chaotic world, are radically free. By their choices, they can create meaning. By their minds and actions, they can take the formlessness of experience and build it into something ordered. They can choose their own values and live and die by them. One person may choose Christianity; another may choose Marxism; another may forge a new religion. To say one position is true or false is irrelevant in a world without ready-made objective structures. Each can be an authentic way of giving meaning to an individual's life.

Existentialism is not simply an eccentric theory found only in the ivory towers of academia. It is everywhere. How many times have you heard statements such as this one: "That may be true for you, but it isn't true for me."' In other words, truth is not objective and binding, applicable to everyone. Instead, it varies from individual to individual according to each person's unique personality. This very difficult philosophical concept has become a truism, something taken for granted by everyone. It does not seem contradictory or unusual. We hear it on soap operas. We say it whenever we meet someone with whom we disagree.

Or, in moral discussions, consider statements such as this: "I don't personally believe in abortion, but I believe other people have the right to choose for themselves." This prochoice position makes moral behavior a matter of the individual's choice. If a person decides not to get an abortion, that is fine. If a person decides to get an abortion, that too is fine. The essential moral requirement is that the woman not be forced to do anything, but be able to have her choice. There is no objective standard of right and wrong that applies to everyone. Values are a matter of making personal decisions, of finding out "what is best for me." The prochoice arguments are a model of existential ethics. Morality is removed from the realm of truth. Ethics have nothing to do with the larger human community, with the solidarity of all human beings. Traditional moralists, on the other hand, speak in terms of objective moral absolutes. Because the two sides in the abortion controversy have entirely different assumptions about the locus of morality, it is little wonder they have such a hard time communicating with each other.

Educators no longer feel confident about teaching moral values, which they have come to think are religious rather than being the common property of all religions and civilizations (as taught in Romans 2:14, 15). Instead of teaching values, they teach values clarification, in which students explore the values they already have and learn to make responsible choices about their sexuality, and so forth.

Modern existential theologians apply situation ethics rather than the Ten Commandments and teach that the events described in the Bible need not have taken place. The objective realm is not important; what is important is the "Christ-event" in a person's life. Faith is redefined as a life of openness to the formless experience and uncertainty of an absurd world. Faith in an objective God and belief in traditional doctrines of Christianity is derided as immature, or even as idolatry.

The artist has a special role in this process of creating meaning. Art is seen as the process of imposing meaning on the chaos of experience. People today often look to artists as the inspired source of values. In their creativity, artists can mesmerize and manipulate their audiences, giving them an ordered experience that, for many, is their only refuge from a meaningless and chaotic world.[3]

According to existentialism, the individual is the creator of meaning. The individual is the source of values. The individual, in other words, is god. This sort of paganism is as old as Eden. The serpent casts doubt on God's Word, questioning both the one moral absolute and the righteous love and authority of God. Satan promises Eve that if she eats the fruit God has forbidden, she will know good and evil for herself, and then "you will be like God" (Genesis 3:4, 5). This, according to Scripture, is the primal sin.

Nature worship is humble; its fault is in minimizing the human being. Self-worship is proud; its fault is in minimizing objective reality. These two schools of paganism flatly contradict each other; yet they often exist together. If human beings are only animals determined by their heredity and environment, as the naturalists say, it is hard to see how they could also be the glorious source of meaning and values, as the humanists say. And yet, humanists will usually assert a naturalistic view of the universe, and naturalists will assert humanistic values. It is as if materialism leaves so little for the individual that it forces the person to glorify the self. That is, after all, the only personal being in the entire universe, as both schools of thought would agree.

THE DEATH OF KNOWLEDGE
Thoughtful people today in almost every field are saying, "there are no absolutes," and "truth is relative." If they really believe that truth is only an enchantment, then the Christian's advantage in the pursuit of knowledge becomes clear.

If you examine anything closely enough, it will seem to dissolve in your hands. A rock seems solid enough. But if you look closer and closer, it becomes a collection of crystals, a set of molecules, a tinker-toy arrangement of atoms, a mass of whirling electrons, a frenetic dance of subatomic particles which themselves turn out to be not solid at all. Instead, they are phases of energy comprehensible only in abstract mathematical formulae. What happened to the rock? Modern physics makes us realize the mystery of creation and the inadequacies of the human mind to fathom the works of God.

Today many people have pushed knowledge so far that they have become skeptical about knowledge itself. We perceive the rock to be solid. That is only because of the make-up of our nervous system. We interpret various sense-impressions according to the channels of our brains. The reality will always elude us. If the human mind constructs its perceptions, then it is the human mind which is the source of any truth that we can know. Today some people are starting to doubt the instrument, to question the very possibility of external knowledge.

In the humanities, what does it mean to speak of human values? If meaning is only in the minds of the beholder, how can we speak of any objective meaning in a novel, a painting, or a poem? Isn't the whole process of teaching the humanities an effort to impose a socially accepted pattern on individual students, of indoctrinating them according to oppressive social standards? What right do we have to say that one idea is any better than others? If truth is relative, what is there to teach? What is there to learn?

Although such radical skepticism is fatal and unanswerable to some educators, it is still possible to be an educator under such assumptions. What happens is that the approach to education becomes radically altered. No longer will a course emphasize a specific content that is handed down and explained to the student. Instead, students are trained in processes and encouraged to develop meanings for themselves. Thus, students are not taught the history of philosophy; rather, they are taught to ask questions and to formulate their own beliefs. Instead of studying literary classics in a literature class, they learn to express themselves and to read literature that is relevant to their own admittedly limited experiences. If you find yourself in a class in which you are not learning anything definite, but instead you are getting in touch with your feelings and relating with other people, do not fear. You are on the cutting edge of modern education.

Such classes are occasionally valuable. There is a problem, though, for the intellectual enterprise as a whole. If there are no objective meanings, and if an individual may choose any meanings he or she wants, objective knowledge can have little importance and will be of little interest to anyone. Many universities have abandoned their required curriculum because there is no longer any consensus about what an educated person should know. Besides, many faculty are saying, who are we to decide what is important for someone else? Students take whatever they want. What they want, of course, is usually something interesting and easy. The most popular classes are often the most entertaining and the least demanding. As a result, "boring" and difficult classes, such as foreign languages, mathematics, and the hard sciences, have trouble finding students.

Things today are not quite as bad as that. A reaction has set in against some of the educational reforms of the 1960s and 1970s. Still, college faculty complain about the poor preparation of their students. Many of them have never accumulated any knowledge on which to build more knowledge. Reading skills are poor. Writing skills are worse. Knowledge of math and science is nonexistent. Their process-orientated education in grade school and high school may have opened their minds, but it has not put anything in.

Such problems point to the real issue: Modern ways of thinking, such as naturalism and existentialism, work against the pursuit of objective knowledge. If the material world is all that exists, why should I study the humanities? If the material world is meaningless, why should I study science? If, as you say, I must create my own meanings and form my own values, why don't you leave me alone?

There was a reason Daniel and his fellow Hebrews were ten times better in their studies than the magicians and the enchanters. It is the same reason modern Christians can outdo their nonbelieving friends on college campuses. The world view of the magicians and the enchanters got in their way of finding truth. In the same way, naturalism and existentialism lead to intellectual and educational dead-ends. A Biblical world view, on the other hand, as the next chapters will show, is open to truth of all kinds—both natural truth and human truth—and offers a way of giving that truth purpose, value, context, and unity.

ELEVEN

CREATION AND CREATIVITY

*I*f the magicians distort nature and the enchanters distort the human being, the sciences and the humanities each must suffer. In contrast, the Biblical view of nature and of the human being provides a world view in which knowledge of all kinds can flourish.

According to Christianity, God created the universe. Moreover, God actually entered this universe, becoming incarnate in Jesus Christ to redeem a fallen world. Because of the doctrine of creation, Christians can never say that anything in the physical world is intrinsically worthless. Because of the doctrine of the Incarnation, Christians can never say that human beings are intrinsically worthless. In these doctrines, a Christian can find a conceptual basis for valuing and pursuing the whole range of human and natural knowledge.

MODELS OF CREATION

The Biblical doctrine that God created the world and everything in it is so familiar that we take this idea for granted. We assume that other religions also believe that their gods created the world in much the same manner. Actually, they do not. The Biblical concept of creation is a radical idea. It is almost unique in world religions and philosophies. The concept of creation has done a great deal to direct the assumptions of Western scholarship. As our culture loses the Biblical assumptions, however, that scholarship will no doubt suffer. To appreciate the Biblical view of creation, it will help to examine the alternatives. It is interesting, for example, to study the view of creation that Daniel would have had to contend with. The Babylonians and other mythological cultures did have stories of the beginning of time, but they were not really creation stories in our sense. Here is the Babylonian creation story (Tiamat is the goddess of Chaos, Mother of All; Marduk is the Champion of the Gods):

> As a man splits a flat fish, Marduk split the body of Tiamat. He set one half of her above as a covering for the heavens; he fixed bolts there so that the floods that are above may not be voided upon the earth, and he stationed a watchman to guard the bolts. Of the other half of Tiamat's body he made the earth. He divided all that was made between Anu, Bel, and Ea—the Heavens, the Earth, and the Abyss. He fixed the stars in their places; he ordained the year and divided it; he caused the Moon God to shine, and he gave him the night for his portion.
>
> Thereafter Marduk devised a plan. He opened his mouth and he spoke to Anu, Bel, and Ea. "My blood I will take and bone I will fashion; I will make man to inhabit the earth so that the service of the Gods may not fail ever." So Marduk spoke, and man began to live upon the earth.[1]

For the Babylonians and other mythic cultures, the physical world is a part of a god's body. As in Eastern philosophies, nature and the gods are continuous. Thus, in mythological cultures, nature becomes sacred and often taboo, not to be touched lest one blaspheme something holy and anger the gods.

Mythological religions are often cyclical, depicting one world which is followed by a new world, which gives way to yet another world. In the Babylonian accounts, something always already exists. For the Greeks, even the gods come and go in cycles, with the original gods, the Titans, being completely displaced by the gods of Mount Olympus. Human beings, in their turn, were created and destroyed and created again in a number of successive cycles, as the Golden Age deteriorated into the Iron Age.[2]

Many modern scientists are falling back into this cyclical view of origins. They speak of the universe expanding until the force of gravity makes it contract, falling in upon itself until it collapses into one white-hot mass. Eventually this mass will explode with another big bang and the universe will again take shape. This process, many have speculated, has been going on and will continue forever and ever. The universe is born and is destroyed and born again in a never-ending and never-beginning cycle.

Eastern religions, now increasingly in vogue in our culture, are somewhat similar, but they teach further that the physical world is an evil illusion from which we must escape. The universe as we perceive it is not real. The world of appearances is described as a spell cast by a demon to deceive and entrap human beings who are now entangled in unreality. Human beings perceive differences in things; actually, reality is all one, a seamless fabric in which nature, human beings, and God are identical. Salvation, in this view, is to escape this world of mere appearances in which things are different and separate from each other, to merge into the cosmic Unity.

"We are all one." "There is a single global consciousness." "We must strive for unity." Such buzz words of the New Age movement, with its roots in Eastern religions, have a great appeal for many people today. Modern materialism and rationalism are rejected in favor of a mellow mysticism which seems so affirmative and loving.

Actually, beneath the appearances created by its glittering generalities and its positive-sounding rhetoric, this sort of philosophy is radically negative and even despairing. If taken seriously, it makes love impossible.[3] Love means a relationship between people who are different from each other. Otherwise, loving someone else means nothing more than loving oneself. If God, other people, pieces of quartz, individual dolphins, different planets, and one's own soul are all the same, then loving God, loving other people, and loving nature become just glorified ways of loving oneself. The whole universe becomes sucked into the black hole of introversion and egotism.

To say everyone and everything is one means that all individual uniqueness must be obliterated. It always seemed to me very glorious that each snowflake, according to the scientists and mathematicians, is, in fact, different from every other snowflake. Eastern and New Age mysticism must concentrate on their unity—that is, on the snowfield's white blankness. Christians believe in the immortality of the soul and the resurrection of the body. That means that individual identities survive after death, not that they are merged into an impersonal unity. Christianity prizes individuality, whereas New Age mysticism, for all of its nonconformist rhetoric, must end in a cosmic sameness.

Non-Western mysticism tends to look inward, not outward. Such a view has important implications for the pursuit of knowledge. It is clear why science and objective research as we know them in the West did not arise in Hindu or Buddhist cultures. They did not lack intelligence or analytical ability. They were simply not interested in the physical world as such. For them, the physical world which we perceive is not real. Insofar as it can be said to exist, it is evil. For those with an Eastern world view, sense-impressions are not reliable. The world is something to escape, not to study. The New Age heirs of this view may cluster around college campuses, but their distrust of science, technology, and reason places them directly at odds with the tradition of Western learning.

THE BIBLICAL MODEL OF THE UNIVERSE

The Bible teaches a view of the creation that is very different conceptually from the mythological, the mystical, and the materialistic world views. According to Scripture, God created everything from nothing. He then proclaimed it "very good."

Thus, the universe is neither the work of a demon nor the work of impersonal natural processes. Everything that exists depends upon the action and the will of a personal God. Behind everything is a Mind. Christians go further: this

Mind is Christ. "In the beginning," says John, "was the Word," the *logos*, the cosmic ordering principle of Greek philosophy, and this Word was made flesh in Jesus (John 1).

> He is the image of the invisible God, the first-born of all creation; for in him all things were created, in heaven and on earth, visible and invisible, whether thrones or dominions or principalities or authorities—all things were created through him and for him. He is before all things, and in him all things hold together. (Colossians 1:15-17)

This means that all things, "visible and invisible," depend upon Christ for their existence. It also means that there is a certain rationality in the universe. Although God's mind is infinitely above ours (which means that His work will at some point prove incomprehensible to our limited reason), we can expect the physical world to be orderly, consistent, and, to some degree, intelligible to us, since we too have minds and personality. All things also are radically compatible to Jesus Christ, in whom "all things hold together." There is thus a certain mysticism in the Christian's affirmation of the physical universe. There is a confidence that whatever is discovered conforms with Jesus Christ and is a manifestation of His will.

God is, however, different from His creation. It is not, strictly speaking, a part of Him, nor do God and all things make up a vast, featureless Unity. God transcends His creation, thereby giving it an existence of its own. We must not "worship and serve the creature rather than the Creator" (Romans 1:25). The physical world, precious as it is, is not sacred as such. We can study it without taboos, confident that it is real and that it will not slip away or change on us like a dream or a mirage.

Moreover, God deliberately created things different from each other. Psalm 104 celebrates the intricate variety of the created order. Cataloguing such things as water, wild donkeys, birds, grass, wine, oil, cedars, storks, mountain goats, badgers, the moon, the sun, lions, whales, and "the sea, great and wide, which teems with things innumerable, living things both small and great [an allusion to microorganisms?]" (vv. 10-25), the Psalm concludes,

> O LORD, how manifold are thy works!
> In wisdom hast thou made them all;
> the earth is full of thy creatures. (Psalm 104:24)

This "manifold" quality of God's creation—its incredible diversity and variety—is an important Biblical teaching. Not only does it set off the Biblical world view from the Eastern insistence on unity, but it also establishes the value of each individual object and each individual person, all unique and valued by God for this uniqueness.

Not only is the creation both orderly and varied, but it is also "good." This too is a crucial and widely neglected teaching of Scripture. After each act of creation, the Bible repeats the refrain: "And God saw that it was good" (Genesis 1:4, 10, 12, 18, 21, 25). Finally God looks upon His entire creation: "And God saw everything that he had made, and behold, it was very good" (Genesis 1:31). Not only is it good, it is *very* good.

God is not here declaring the creation valuable just because He made it and because it conforms to His wishes. The Bible goes further: God "saw" that it was good. In other words, there is something in creation that is good in itself. God put the goodness there, in His work, but it is objectively present. God Himself recognizes and responds to the goodness that He sees.

Certainly sin has spoiled this created goodness and has tragically disrupted the whole creation. The Fall embraces not only human beings, but the whole natural order over which human beings had been given dominion. Yet, there is a primal goodness that still inheres in everything that God has made.

This is underscored in a very important passage in 1 Timothy 4. Warning about the false teachers who will arise, St. Paul says that they will forbid marriage and insist on abstinence from certain foods. (He would be referring to the Gnostic heretics who shared basically the Eastern world view with its rejection of the physical world.) He describes such rejection of sexuality and of the pleasures of eating as "pretentions" and as "doctrines of demons." Why does St. Paul react so strongly against such denials of the flesh? Because "God created" such things "to be received with thanksgiving by those who believe and know the truth" (vv. 1-3).

> For everything created by God is good, and nothing is to be rejected if it is received with thanksgiving; for then it is consecrated by the word of God and prayer. (vv. 4, 5)

"Everything created by God is good." What does that exclude? Only sin, which, as St. Augustine explains, is a lack, an emptiness, an absence of God and the goodness that He created. What is real, however, is so because God made it just the way it is. Therefore, it is good.

Sexuality, for example, is designed by God and is thus good in itself. People can use sexuality in unlawful ways to commit sexual sins. This is evil precisely because it violates God's good design. Sinners turn something life-giving into something barren and infertile; they turn something designed for love into something manipulative and exploiting. The problem is not sexuality, but the lack of full sexuality as God intended in its created wholeness. Human beings can and do manipulate and spoil the created order for their own sinful egos, but sinfulness resides not in the external created world but in the human heart (see Matthew 15:10-20).

Furthermore, because of this doctrine of creation, St. Paul points out, "nothing is to be rejected." Nothing. A person who believes the Bible dare not reject anything. Dirt, rocks, worms; amoeba, electrons, galaxies; nitrogen, energy, genetics; music, language, colors—all must be affirmed. Moreover, it follows that a person who believes the Bible dare not reject the study of any of God's creations. Biology, geology, physics, astronomy, linguistics, and all other sciences simply explore and bear testimony to what God has made.

Certainly, modern scientists tend to exclude God. There are other world views besides the Eastern, mythological, and Biblical, and they are put forward as being more congenial to the pursuit of knowledge. Yet, even modern scientific materialism can be seen an aberration, a falling away from the Biblical world view which it still depends upon. Materialism itself presupposes many of the Biblical assumptions. No one could have dreamed that the physical world was knowable and consistent, were it not for the Biblical doctrine of creation. No one would have bothered to spend so much time analyzing the trivia of nature if they did not believe that it had some value in itself.[4]

As many drift farther and farther away from our culture's Biblical heritage, I suspect there will be a corresponding decline in science. Already many are questioning whether the objective world is knowable after all. Even more are questioning the value of pure research. Meanwhile, the popular mind is returning to mythology—to horoscopes and herbal magic, to old superstitions and occultism dressed in the garb of science—for example, UFO's and ESP. It is time for Christians to reclaim their interest in God's creation.

THE IMAGE OF GOD

One other part of the doctrine of creation deserves special emphasis. Human beings, according to the Bible, are created in the image of God (Genesis 1:26). Thus, human beings have enormous value and powers. The Biblical doctrine that human beings have value has rich implications for the study of the humanities.

To say that human beings were made in the image of God means many things. God is personal; therefore, human beings are personal. God has a mind, a consciousness, the ability to reason and to distinguish between right and wrong. God has a personality. So do we. All of these faculties and powers that we enjoy and take for granted come from and point to God. In Him, they are perfect. They are infinite, without bounds. In us, they are highly limited and, worse, distorted by sin. Some say the divine image is totally effaced by the primal sin. Nevertheless, our God-created human nature was not totally erased by the Fall. In fact, the Bible holds up our creation in the image of God as the reason human life is sacred. The Biblical teaching on murder sees it as blasphemy no less than cruelty, an assault on the image of God Himself (Genesis 9:6).

Christians must honor the divine image in every person they see. Non-Biblical world views popular today tend to value people on the basis of their use to society, or their physical attractiveness, or their ability to reason, or their ability to pursue a meaningful life. Hence the unusual trendiness of the euthanasia movement and the outrages against the handicapped, the mentally retarded, the aged, the very sick, and the not yet born. If a child is unwanted, or has an extremely low IQ, or is very ugly to look at, it is better for that child to not live. If a person lacks human dignity or is seen as a vegetable (no Christian should speak of a human being in that way), then it is better to put him out of his misery.

Such views are other examples of the neo-pagan revival. Euthanasia and abortion were quite common in the ancient world and for the same reasons given today. The Hebrews, on the other hand, and the early Church vigorously opposed such practices.[5] For them, the value of a human being's life does not depend upon whether the person is a benefit or a burden to society, or whether he or she is beautiful or ugly, intelligent or retarded. As the bearer of the divine image, uniquely created and loved by God, each person has value, worth, and stature that can never be taken away. This stature resides not in the circumstances and appearances of this changeable world, but is transcendent, grounded in God Himself.

This view of human beings flowered in Western civilization, bearing fruit in concepts such as individualism and inalienable rights. As the Biblical view declines in our culture, the rejection of human rights and the decay of individualism are already upon us. Marxist countries self-consciously suppress these concepts. In the Western democracies, they are being trivialized. Individualism has come to mean the willingness to follow yet another mass, commercialized, collective fashion. A person now is individualistic because of peer pressure. The modern individualist is less interested in identity and integrity than the all-consuming demand to do what he wants, which means in practice to follow his worst instincts and mass-stimulated desires. The term *rights* has become another glittering generality, a buzz-word to be attached to any and every cause to coerce noncritical acceptance—abortion rights, sexual rights, animal rights. The nobility of "the right of free expression" is used now mainly to protect pornographers. Divorced from its theological context, the term is becoming an absurdity that is held on to and invoked with superstitious tenacity. True individualism and human rights cannot last long at this rate.

The Biblical thinker, on the other hand, has a basis for insisting upon human worth. Each individual is precious. Moreover, in bearing an immortal soul, each individual is eternal. The infinite destiny of each individual, whether in Heaven or in Hell, means that each person, no matter how lowly, will outlast societies and civilizations, which will all pass away.[6] There are mysteries in each person—the mystery of iniquity and the mystery of righteousness. Every person, known in depth, is inexhaustible. That God Himself became a human being in the mystery of the Incarnation charges human life with an even greater significance.

The study of human beings—their makeup, their history, their accomplishments—must always have a special fascination for the Christian. As God's richest and most complex creation, human beings bear both the image of God and the curse of sin. The mysteries of the human mind are a vast, nearly unexplored landscape. Psychology explores how these creatures think. Philosophy explores what they think. The social sciences explore how they live. History explores the record of what human beings have done on earth, their monstrous crimes and their dazzling achievements.

The doctrines of the creation and the image of God are especially revealing when considering the arts—music, painting, sculpture, literature, and the rest. As many wise Christians have observed, being created in God's image means that human beings also have the ability to create.[7] Just as God can create a universe, human beings, on a far smaller scale of course, can create beautiful sounds, physical structures, visual images, and imaginary worlds. The human urge to create both points to and comes from the Divine Artist who is the model and source of all creativity.

The study and practice of the arts is thus a particularly worthy calling for the Christian. Materialists have problems justifying art—they have little basis for concepts such as beauty, objective form, and creation for its own sake. Why bother with something so impractical? It is true that the neo-pagans are turning art into a religion, as in the old days. Art is often described as "the source of values" and is treated as something quite sacred and esoteric. Idolatrous art, though, has always tended to be stuffy, pretentious, and even conservative, as hard as it tries to be radical. The Biblical view of art is far more liberating.

God gave to a craftsman named Bezalel the gifts necessary to create the art of the Tabernacle. These gifts—the Holy Spirit, ability, intelligence, knowledge, craftsmanship, and teaching (Exodus 35:30—36:1)—together make up the capacity to be an artist. Christians should claim them for what they are. Christians should compose and perform music, they should paint pictures and abstract designs, they should write poetry and novels. They should also study the arts because in so doing they are gazing into the heart of the mystery of creation.[8]

There is a great deal of discussion today about secular humanism, the exaltation of human beings coupled with the rejection of religious faith. Secular humanism is bound to fail. Faith in human nature or the human spirit is certainly a superstitious and fanatical belief.[9] There is so little evidence, based on observation alone, that human beings are as wonderful as secular humanists say they are. Secular humanism ignores sin and thereby ignores a large part of what it means to be human. Ironically, it promotes sexual freedom, abortion, euthanasia, and suicide, all in the name of human dignity. Humanism exalts humanity in a superficial way only to drag it down and even kill it, because it lacks any transcendent reference-point that alone can truly establish human worth. The problem with secular humanism is that it can so easily become inhuman. Christian humanism, on the other hand, is human because it is Christian.

Christians in the humanities, with their concept of the image of God, and Christians in the sciences, with their concept of God's creation, should be "ten times better" than those in the humanities and the sciences today who are floundering for a ground to stand on. The doctrine of creation unites both an interest in the objective world of nature and an interest in the subjective world of human beings, exalting both the creation as it is and the whole principle of creativity.

Christianity goes further: The mystery of the Incarnation brings together the doctrine of nature and the doctrine of humanity. It also establishes both the limits and the glory of nature and human nature. Because human beings have by their sin turned the image of God into a monstrosity, and because the creation itself is warped by their Fall, God Himself, the Second Person of the Trinity, has entered His creation and become a man, experiencing everything that human beings experience (except for sin), including death itself (Hebrews 2:14; 4:15), to restore what He has made. The material world and human life look very different to Christians now that the Son of God has been here. Because of Christ, Christians should have "ten times" the love of life and the love of the physical world than those who are dead in their sins. They should have "ten times" the interest in the details of what God has done in creation and in what human beings are capable of doing. They should have "ten times" the zeal in learning.

CHRISTIANITY AS AN INTELLECTUAL FRAMEWORK

*T*he most common criticism of Christian scholars is that their belief in dogmas inhibits the open-minded search for truth. You already know what you believe, they say. You already think you have all of the answers. Why engage in study and research? Won't you simply try to fit whatever you find into your predetermined beliefs? Even if you are more honest than that, isn't your intellectual search over before it begins? Doesn't your belief in settled religious dogmas stifle the open-ended inquiry that is at the heart of the academic enterprise?

These are important questions, and Christians in academia must continually face them. I would argue, however, that dogmatic Christian theology, far from stifling the pursuit of knowledge, actually can provide a framework for acquiring and for integrating new knowledge. In fact, the Christian way of thinking is far better (ten times better) than secular relativism as a framework for learning new ideas.

BOTH/AND: THE PARADOXES OF CHRISTIANITY
A paradox is a statement that contains two apparently contradictory ideas, both of which taken together are true. "I was so happy it made me cry." "You only hate the ones you love." "She was so popular that no one liked her." These are paradoxes of human emotions, seemingly contradictory, but everyone knows what they mean and would probably accept

them as true. Human beings tend to be paradoxical. Physical
reality is also paradoxical, as modern scientists are just discovering. "Light is both a particle and a wave." "Objects are both
at rest and in constant motion." "Human beings are determined by their environment, but they are also free to make
their own decisions."

Such ideas go against simplistic common sense, but this
is because of the clumsiness of human logic. They do not
really violate the law of contradiction. They are coherent,
rational ideas. They are just very complex and difficult to
fathom for the limited human mind. Truth, when we understand it deeply, often turns out to be a paradox.

Christianity has always presented its key doctrines as a
series of paradoxes. Jesus Christ is true God and true man.
God is a unity of three distinct Persons. Human beings are
toally depraved sinners, yet they are valuable images of God.
To be orthodox is to accept paradox.

Rationalism tends to think in terms of either/or. The
Greeks and their intellectual heirs tend to think in terms of a
golden mean, a compromise between two opposites. Christianity tends to think in terms of both/and.

Consider, for example, the question of the identity of
Jesus Christ. The rationalists say that He is either God or
man, one or the other. The Gnostics believe that He is God
but not man; the Arians believe that He is man but not God.
Both work with rationalist categories—"either/or," one or the
other, take your pick. Another alternative, familiar to Greek
paganism, would be to forge a golden mean, a compromise
between extremes. In this view, Jesus Christ is half-God and
half-man, a demigod such as Hercules. The early Church,
however, rejected both Greek philosophy and Greek mythology and insisted that Jesus is *both* God *and* man. In the
wonderfully precise words of the old creeds, Jesus is "very
God" and "very Man." He is extremely human; He is extremely divine. Any other view denies the mysteries of the
Incarnation and the Redemption, in which God became a
human being, sharing our full humanness, in order to bear
the sins of the world, becoming our mediator, substitute, and
advocate.

The same patterns of thinking are evident in the debates about the Trinity. The Father, Son, and Holy Spirit are not three separate beings, nor are they simply different names for a single deity. Rather, they are three separate Persons who constitute an absolute unity. The Father is different from the Son who is different from the Holy Spirit, and yet their unity is so intimate and absolute that they are one God. The Godhead itself is a personal relationship, so that it is possible to say, "God is love" (1 John 4:8). The Father, Son, and Holy Spirit are distinct, and yet they are one. According to Scripture, as explained in the Athanasian Creed, "confounding the persons"—denying the uniqueness of each of the three—and "dividing the substance"—separating the three into three separate gods—are both departures from the Christian faith.

The same pattern inheres in the doctrine of the human being. Human beings are desperate sinners, evil to the core, deserving only eternal punishment in Hell. At the same time, they are made in the image of God, who loves them so much that the Father gave up His Son to bring them to Heaven. Human beings are radically limited and yet they are radically gifted. A Christian is, at the same time, both a sinner and a saint, a creature of dust and a child of God, a miserably depraved animal capable of the most brutal crimes and an heir of righteousness called to self-sacrifice and love.

Is Christianity optimistic or pessimistic? Both! It can be more pessimistic than the bleakest existentialist in denouncing the evils of the world, the fall of civilization, the futility of human striving, and the destiny of the human race in Hell. It can, at the same time, be more optimistic than the most starry-eyed dreamer in its insistence that "all things work together for good" (Romans 8:28, KJV), that Christ will triumph, that an eternity of joy exists in Heaven. Christians teach both God's judgment and His mercy, His holiness and His love, His severity and His grace.

G. K. Chesterton has provocatively explored this paradoxical quality of Christianity. He noticed how Christianity has always scorned suicides but honored martyrs; how it has promoted both celibacy and families; how it sometimes seems warlike and sometimes seems pacifistic; how it has always promoted both fasting and feasting. It takes two opposite extremes and exalts them both. "We want not an amalgam or compromise," concludes Chesterton, "but both things at the top of their energy; love and wrath both burning."[1] This quality of Christianity makes it liberating, flexible, and dynamic:

> St. Francis, in praising all good, could be a more shouting optimist than Walt Whitman. St. Jerome, in denouncing all evil, could paint the world blacker than Schopenhauer. Both passions were free because both were kept in their place. . . . By defining its main doctrine, the Church not only kept seemingly inconsistent things side by side, but, what was more, allowed them to break out in a sort of artistic violence . . . things that are to virtue what the crimes of Nero are to vice. The spirits of indignation and of charity took terrible and attractive forms, ranging from that monkish fierceness that scourged like a dog the first and greatest of the Plantagenets, to the sublime pity of St. Catherine, who, in the official shambles, kissed the bloody head of the criminal. . . .
>
> It is true that the historic Church has at once emphasized celibacy and emphasized the family; has at once (if one may put it so) been fiercely for having children and fiercely for not having children. It has kept them side by side like two strong colours, red and white, like the red and white upon the shield of St. George. It has always had a healthy hatred of pink. It hates that combination of two colours which is the feeble expedient of the philosophers. It hates that evolution of black into white which is tantamount to a dirty gray. . . . It is not a mixture like russet or purple; it is rather like a shot silk, for a shot silk is always at right angles, and is in the pattern of a cross.[2]

Christianity is thus radically comprehensive. It embraces everything, from one pole of experience to the other. It is also dynamic. It resists the simplistic pat answer which secularists are always looking for. What it affirms and what it rejects are always surprises to the world. It dances through the history of Western thought.

YES/BUT: THE FLEXIBILITY OF THE CHRISTIAN MIND

Because Christianity is so comprehensive and open to paradox, it is very flexible intellectually. This does not mean compromising the absolutes of Biblical doctrine. Rather, by accepting those doctrines, it is possible to accommodate and make sense of a wide range of ideas, evidence, and experiences.

This paradoxical play of the mind, which Christianity encourages, is open to truth wherever it may be found, but it refuses to take one limited perception as an absolute. It accepts reason without making limited human reason the judge of all truth. It accepts scientific methodology without reducing the universe to a test tube. Because it teaches that human beings can know the world but are very, very limited, Christianity can accept the discoveries of reason and science (even those which seem to contradict each other) without seeing them as final answers.

Christian doctrine provides a very helpful way of aligning knowledge, of seeing how different insights and discoveries fit together. Notice how Christianity can both accept and qualify the commonplaces of modern thought:

Human beings are insignificant. We are adrift in an infinite universe, briefly occupying a tiny planet circling a minor star in a corner of an insignificant galaxy. Yes. "When I look at thy heavens, the work of thy fingers, the moon and the stars which thou hast established, what is man that thou art mindful of him, and the son of man that thou dost care for him?" (Psalm 8:3, 4). The Book of Ecclesiastes and the Book of Job affirm the vanity and futility of human strivings, the smallness of human life and the absurdity of our pretensions to greatness. "For we are but of yesterday, and know nothing, for our days on earth are a shadow" (Job 8:9).

Christians understand the truth of human insignificance and know how to relate such insights to the world view

of modern scientists and philosophers. We are nothing compared to the infinity of God. But that is not the whole story.
The meditation in Psalm 8 on the smallness of human beings
in light of the galaxies is immediately followed by a meditation on their greatness through God's grace: "Yet thou has
made him little less than God, and dost crown him with glory
and honor. Thou hast given him dominion over the works of
thy hands; thou hast put all things under his feet" (vv. 5, 6).
Astronomy may point to the physical smallness of human
beings, but it itself exemplifies the vastness of the human
mind, which is part of the incredible "dominion" God has
chosen to give to these seemingly insignificant creatures. Yes,
we are insignificant, but we are also crowned with glory and
honor. Yes, we are small, but we are also great. Yes, our lives
are short, but our souls are immortal.

If one branch of secularism stresses the insignificance of
humanity, another branch stresses the opposite: *Human beings are the source of all values and meaning. Human freedom,
dignity, and individualism must be nourished. People must be free
to grow, to develop, and to express themselves until they find
perfect fulfillment, satisfying all their desires in a society based on
love and harmony.* Yes. Christians, like the humanists, value
humanity and agree with the greatness and the reality of
human rights, accomplishments, and values. We too are uto-
pians, looking forward to a Kingdom where the lion lies
down with the lamb and all of our yearnings are fulfilled.

But we think the humanists neglect the reality and the
enormity of human sin. Satisfying all human desires, searching for individual fulfillment, and making the self the source
of all values have historically issued in wars, selfishness, conflict, brutality, and oppression. Human achievements include
Buchenwald as well as the great works of art. A utopia based
only on human nature will be a crude parody of Hell. In fact,
the future utopia in which the autonomous self will find
perfect fulfillment is Hell. For Christians, true humanism
must be based on the one Person who was truly human, just
as He was truly divine. The way to utopia lies through Him
and lies beyond this world. It is not the Kingdom of Man—

we have had enough of that—but the Kingdom of God.

Human beings are determined by their environment and by their genes. Individual freedom is an illusion. We cannot escape the influence of our families and our societies. Yes. Christians can agree with the social scientists that we are, in a sense, determined by our innate makeup or by our environmental influences and that we are not as free as we like to think we are. We believe in original sin. Going back to Adam and Eve, the gene-pool and all human communities have been sick. We cannot escape our human condition. We cannot escape our propensity to sin. We were born to it. We were taught to sin. Our very wills are in bondage. We believe also in the positive workings of families and communities. God established human families as His means of nurturing and forming His children. Because we are social creatures, He bonds us into societies and engrafts us into His Church.

But we also believe in moral responsibility. We sin, but we do so as free moral agents. Other people may be involved in our sinfulness, but we are willing co-conspirators. God can deliver us from our bondage to sin. It is difficult, but we can resist our societies, peer groups, and even our own upbringing and psychological makeup to do what we know is right. We exist in societies, but we also exist as individual, immortal souls, made uniquely by God who values us for our own sakes. We have transcendent human rights. Since each of us will live forever, we will outlast human institutions, which should never be absolute nor usurp individual freedoms.

Notice the pattern: Yes . . . But . . . Christians can affirm various assertions and pieces of evidence from the scientists, humanists, and social scientists. We can place these pieces of knowledge in the larger context of Biblical truth and learn from them. We also, however, recognize them as partial, qualifying them and moving on.

The scientist's belief that human beings are very insignificant in the universe contradicts the humanist's assertions about the importance of human beings. The social scientist's determinism contradicts the humanist's emphasis on individualism and freedom. Simply in their own terms, they cannot all be right. Yet, Christianity offers a perspective that can affirm the truth in each position, while balancing it in a more comprehensive vision.

CHRISTIAN SKEPTICISM

This Christian habit of mind combines openness to truth with skepticism. As such, it is an excellent mind-set for the pursuit of knowledge.

The common secularist view that truth is relative cultivates skepticism, but it is not, in the final analysis, open to truth. It denies that there is truth. The learner is never satisfied with the static knowledge of the past, but can only acquire insights that must themselves be superseded as static and thus invalid. Relativism, with its skepticism for its own sake, calls itself into question—"What is the point of all of this research if what I am saying is just as relative and changeable as what I am criticizing?" Skepticism is important for learning, but without some commitment to the objective existence of truth, it becomes like the "universal wolf" in Shakespeare, which devours the whole world and then must consume itself (*Troilus and Cressida*, I.iii.121-124).

Christian skepticism, on the other hand, sees knowledge in terms of ever larger circles of meaning, related finally to the revealed truths of Scripture. It is not content with an isolated discovery of a particular philosopher or a particular century. For Flannery O'Connor, "What kept me a skeptic in college was precisely my Christian faith. It always said: wait, don't bite on this, get a wider picture, continue to read."[3] In a letter to a college student on the verge of giving up his faith, this great modern Christian novelist pointed out that faith "is more valuable, more mysterious, altogether more immense than anything you can learn or decide upon in college. Learn what you can, but cultivate Christian skepticism. It will keep you free—not free to do anything you please, but free to be formed by something larger than your own intellect or the intellects of those around you."[4]

Christians will thus often find themselves to be gadflies in their fields. They will not accept the conventional wisdom of their field, nor hold to all of its values. Their attitudes and practices will be similar to those of Blaise Pascal, the mathematical genius and Christian thinker whose explorations of the paradoxes of the human soul show the Christian mind at its best. Referring to his planned defense of the Christian faith to human beings in all of their contradictions, Pascal makes the following resolution: "If he vaunts himself,/I abase him./If he abases himself, I vaunt him,/and gainsay him always/until he understands/that he is a monster beyond understanding."[5]

Today many thinkers will "vaunt" humanity, trying to build a faith in human beings alone. When this happens, the Christian thinker must "abase" humanity, revealing its limits and the enormity of its sins. Other thinkers today "abase" humanity, denying human uniqueness and value, rejecting human rights and tearing down human dignity. When this happens, the Christian thinker must "vaunt" humanity, insisting upon the infinite value and potential of every immortal soul. Every human being is "a monster"—not in the sense of Frankenstein or Dracula, but a monster in the sense of being abnormal and unnatural. The Christian thinker must lead people to "understand" the paradox that they are "beyond understanding."

Pascal is advocating what Neil Postman calls a "thermostatic" education. According to Postman, successful education should counter and thereby balance the dominant trends in a society. If a society is very conservative, closed, and static, it is the job of education to challenge that conservatism and to open up its students to change. If, however, a society is very dynamic, open, and changing (as is the case today), it is the job of education to challenge that dynamism, to affirm tradition and to be conservative. Like a thermostat turning on the heat when the room is too cold and turning on the air conditioning when the room is too hot, education must always oppose the dominant trends in order to maintain a healthy culture.[6] Likewise, Christians should be cultural and intellectual thermostats, exulting in opposition, iconoclasm, and new balancing insights.

This is an exciting time to be a Christian. The old materialisms are starting to fall apart. People are rethinking their assumptions. The radicals have become so radical that they are even casting doubt on their radicalism. In the intellectual ferment of this late twentieth century, Christians can speak with clarity and conviction, and there will be people who will listen.

The Christian style of thinking, with its tolerance for paradox, with its combination of openness and skepticism, seems especially suited to the intellectual issues of the day. Modern physics, for example, demands the logic of paradox. Refuting the assumptions of nineteenth-century materialism, it speaks of light being both a particle and a wave, of matter as something almost spiritual, of cause and effect practically being turned upside down. Some Christian scholars believe these discoveries are subversive to Christianity. I cannot agree. It is the secular rationalists who need to be on the run from such mind-boggling research, not believers in the Holy Trinity and in the Light of the World. It is the materialists who have the narrow, closed minds that need to be opened up to the mysteries all around them.

Theologians have always spoken of the limits of reason, teaching that spiritual realities elude the reach of human logic alone, that we must be dependent upon the revelation of God's Word—not our twisted, fallen minds—to discern the truths of an infinite God. Christians must beware of putting too much confidence in their own understanding. It may be also that modern physics is bumping against the limits of human reason, finding reality more complex and intricate than the human mind can fathom.

In terms of the old theological controversy, we must not try to "understand in order to believe"; rather, like St. Anselm, we must "believe in order to understand." When the truth of God's Word is accepted by faith, every other bit of knowledge falls into place, like pieces of a puzzle when the pattern is solved or the tumblers clicking in a lock when we find the right key. The paradox that we can only understand the world by accepting the truth of a faith that defies our full understanding is demonstrated by Chesterton. He points out that we cannot stare into the brightness of the sun, and yet it is by the light of the sun that we see everything else. "The one created thing which we cannot look at is the one thing in the light of which we look at everything."[7] He then turns to a symbol that is even more profound:

> The cross, though it has at its heart a collision and a contradiction, can extend its four arms forever without altering its shape. Because it has a paradox in its centre it can grow without changing. The circle [of rationalism and Eastern Religions] returns upon itself and is bound. The cross opens its arms to the four winds; it is a signpost for free travellers.[8]

THIRTEEN

CONCLUSION: LOVING GOD WITH ALL YOUR MIND

"*H*ear, O Israel: The LORD our God is one LORD; and you shall love the LORD your God with all your heart, and with all your soul, and with all your might" (Deuteronomy 6:4, 5). This profound teaching of the Old Testament through Moses is referred to by Christ as the greatest commandment of them all. Interestingly, when Jesus cites this Scripture, he adds to it another way of loving God:

> And one of the scribes came up and heard them disputing with one another, and seeing that he answered them well, asked him, "Which commandment is the first of all?" Jesus answered, "The first is, 'Hear, O Israel: The Lord our God, the Lord is one; and you shall love the Lord your God with all your heart, and with all your soul, and with all your mind, and with all your strength.' " (Mark 12:28-30)

Interestingly, Jesus adds, "with all your mind."

Loving God with all your heart must refer to loving God with the will and the emotions. Loving God with all your soul must refer to the personal relationship with Him which comes through faith. Loving God with all your strength must refer to serving Him in our actions and good works. What does loving God with all your mind involve?

Most simply, it must mean thinking about God—being
conscious of Him in everyday living, contemplating His presence and His goodness, saturating our minds with His Word.
This is clear from the rest of the passage from Deuteronomy,
which our Lord is no doubt alluding to:

> And these words which I command you this day
> shall be upon your heart; and you shall teach them
> diligently to your children, and shall talk of them
> when you sit in your house, and when you walk by
> the way, and when you lie down, and when you rise.
> (6:6-9)

This text, commanding that God's Word be taught to children and that it be discussed by adults, is the foundation of
Christian education. Loving God with the mind is thus con-
nected to teaching and to learning.

Jesus goes even further. He tells us to love God with
"all" your mind. In other words, everything the mind is
capable of doing is to be devoted to loving God. It would
seem then that if your mind can spin out complex mathematical calculations, you are to love God in mathematics. If your
mind can plan a business, design a building, analyze a novel,
understand a philosophical problem, or imagine a story, you
are to love God in your planning, designing, analyzing, understanding, or imagining. When Jesus says "all" the mind,
He is claiming every mental faculty we have.

When he says "all *your*" mind, He is applying this claim
in a very personal way. Not everyone has the same ability.
Someone who is physically handicapped may not have the
same physical "strength" that a star athlete does. That does
not matter. Whether it means serving God from a hospital
bed or from an Olympic pavilion, both are called to love God
with all of their strength. In the same way, "all your mind"
encompasses a wide range of talents and abilities. Some minds
are gifted in the sciences; some in the arts. Some minds are
oriented to academia and higher education; some are not. No
one set of talents is better than any other. The point is, God
demands all that we can do and all that we can think.

The whole educational enterprise, for a Christian,

should be caught up in the desire to love God with all of the mind. The whole process of curiosity, questioning, and discovery can be a journey, full of wonder and praise, into the mind of God, who created everything. Whatever can be studied, whether human nature or the physical universe, is what it is because God willed it and made it. To uncover the hidden laws that govern matter, to disclose the patterns of subatomic particles, to discover how human beings grow and interact, to discern an underlying pattern in history or in astronomy—all of these amount to nothing less than discovering God's will.

Just as God is inexhaustible, knowledge is inexhaustible. Our curiosity and understanding can never be fully satisfied in our earthly lives. As thirst is evidence for water, our yearning for knowledge points to Heaven, in which all desires will be fully satisfied: "Now I know in part; then I shall understand fully, even as I have been fully understood" (1 Corinthians 13:12).

PRAISE

Loving God with all of the mind means to praise Him for everything that is learned. It is to love God for all of His works. It is to cultivate the sensitivity and the excitement of the Psalmist, who exults in "the works of the Lord":

> Praise the LORD.
> I will give thanks to the LORD with my whole heart, in the company of the upright, in the congregation.
> Great are the works of the LORD, studied by all who have pleasure in them.
> Full of honor and majesty is his work, and his righteousness endures for ever.
> He has caused his wonderful works to be remembered. . . .
> He has shown his people the power of his works, in giving them the heritage of the nations.
> The works of his hands are faithful and just; all his precepts are
> trustworthy,
> they are established for ever and ever. . . .

> The fear of the LORD is the beginning of wisdom; a
> good understanding have all those who practice
> it.
> His praises are for ever! (Psalm 111:1-4, 6, 7, 10)

Referring both to God's deeds of salvation and to His activities
in creation, the Psalmist sees God's works as not only consistent and dependable, but also as "wonderful." They are things
to remember, to pass down from generation to generation.
Verse 2 is the perfect text for any student: "*Great are the works
of the LORD, studied by all who have pleasure in them.*" The
pleasure of learning, which impels people to study God's works
more and more deeply, is really finding pleasure in God.

Verse 10 also is a key text for the Christian student:
"The fear of the LORD is the beginning of wisdom" (see also
Proverbs 1:7). Fearing God is not the end of wisdom, but it is
the beginning. A person who fears God can be opened up to
vast and dizzying heights of knowledge. Those who "practice"
the fear of God can have "a good understanding" of everything.

GIRD UP YOUR MINDS
Such understanding is valuable in itself, but this is a sinful
and fallen world. As such, Christians need to use their minds
for another reason.

Peter addresses his first epistle to "the exiles" (1 Peter
1:1). The early Christians saw themselves as being in the same
position as the Hebrews after the Babylonian conquest. In
these last days, Christians are dispersed throughout a world
that is hostile to Christ and to His people. The term "Babylon" was applied to the Roman Empire (1 Peter 5:13), and was
extended in prophecy to the world-system of the Antichrist
(Revelation 18).

Peter reminds his readers that their faith will be tested
and that they will experience suffering. He stresses their
privilege as God's people and their joy in Christ. He concludes that Christians need to cultivate certain attitudes:

> Therefore gird up your minds, be sober, set your
> hope fully upon the grace that is coming to you at

the revelation of Jesus Christ. As obedient children,
do not be conformed to the passions of your former
ignorance, but as he who called you is holy, be holy
yourselves in all your conduct. . . . conduct yourselves with fear throughout the time of your exile.
(1 Peter 1:13-15, 17)

Living as exiles in this sinful world, Christians must be both
hopeful and obedient. They must take their plight seriously.
To survive in this new Babylon, you must, he says, "gird up
your minds." The figure of speech is one of preparation, of
getting ready for battle, as when a warrior puts on his armor
and buckles on his sword (cf. Ephesians 6:14). Peter is saying
that we must prepare our minds. This girded up mind is in
contrast to "the passions of your former ignorance." Ignorance breeds sin. The Christian must battle sin and faithless-
ness with a fully prepared mind.

Peter is not writing about education as such, but the
principle still holds. Education means preparing the mind.
For a Christian, the pursuit of education can be a means of
"girding up your mind," of exercising, training, and strength-
ening it for ministry in a sinful and spiritually dangerous
world.

This is especially important today. Our society is very
well-educated and sophisticated, but it has lost its moorings
in Biblical truth. In addressing a group of Christian students
at Oxford University, C. S. Lewis spoke of the urgency of
Christians participating in the intellectual battles:

If all the world were Christian, it might not matter
if all the world were educated. But, as it is, a cultural
life will exist outside the Church whether it exists
inside or not. To be ignorant and simple now—not
to be able to meet the enemies on their own
ground—would be to throw down our weapons,
and to betray our uneducated brethren who have,
under God, no defence but us against the intellectual attacks of the heathen. Good philosophy must
exist, if for no other reason, because bad philosophy
needs to be answered.[1]

Christians with academic gifts need to use them to defend the Christians who do not have them. It is precisely because there is so much error in the world today that there is such a great need for truth. "The learned life then is, for some, a duty," concludes Lewis. "At the moment it looks as if it were your duty."[2]

THROUGH THE DARK AGES

After Rome, that second Babylon, fell to the barbarians and to its own vices, Western civilization endured an era of chaos and ignorance. These Dark Ages (not to be confused as they often are with the Middle Ages) were times in which knowledge and learning seemed to be almost stamped out. The Vandals burned the libraries. Reading became almost a lost art. The ancient languages were forgotten. People were concerned with little else than pleasure and survival. Europe was numbed with intellectual apathy.

Yet learning survived. The heritage of Greek culture and Roman law was not forgotten. The masterpieces of literature and philosophy, the great achievements, discoveries, and history of the past were preserved, cherished, and passed on to the succeeding generations, to the High Middle Ages, to the Renaissance, and, eventually, to us.

What brought learning through these Dark Ages? Why was the accumulated knowledge of millennia not lost? Not much is left of Nebuchadnezzar's Babylon, only what archaeologists have dug up. Modern linguists have finally learned how to decipher the cuneiform writing of Babylon, but until that happened, the language and thus the culture faded from history. Why did the same thing not happen to the Greco-Roman civilization? Why did we not have to start all over?

The reason is simple: Learning was kept alive by the Christian Church. In the monasteries, which were built like fortresses to keep out the ravaging barbarians, the monks were copying out books. The Bible and St. Augustine, but also histories and philosophy, Virgil and Cicero, texts of medicine and biology, poetry and engineering—all were copied out in longhand, read and discussed, preserved and stored for a more settled age to come which could use them. In the parish churches, the priest and those whom he would teach kept alive the art of reading, out of their devotion to the Word of God.

When I look at the modern world, I sometimes wonder if we are not slipping into a new Dark Age. There are new Vandals who are trashing the great values and achievements of our civilization. There is a new barbarism which seems to hate ideas and beauty, which scorns order and objective values. People entertain themselves by watching chain-saw massacres at the movies. Unrestrained brutality is seen as great fun. Recreational violence, anti-intellectualism, and a mad lust for pleasure are spreading like an oil-slick through Western culture. Even our thinkers seem demoralized and undisciplined. The intellectual elite themselves are decadent, lawless, and increasingly trivial. As Yeats puts it,

> Things fall apart; the center cannot hold;
> Mere anarchy is loosed upon the world,
> The blood-dimmed tide is loosed, and everywhere
> The ceremony of innocence is drowned;
> The best lack all conviction, while the worst
> Are filled with passionate intensity.[3]

If we are going through another Dark Age, it may be that learning will again survive, as it always has, in the Christian Church. I have a vision of Christians meeting together to discuss fine points of theology and other ideas when no one else is interested in abstract thinking. I picture the Christian colleges—I have not said enough about them as alternatives to secular academia—as enclaves of the liberal arts while the public colleges have all become sophisticated trade schools. I imagine Christians reading their Bibles and other books, while everyone else is watching television.

If Christ delays His coming, and if the Church refuses to conform to the trends of the world, it may be that Christians, as they have in the past, will help usher in a new Renaissance, a flowering of the arts and sciences, a renewal of Western culture, and a revival of Biblical spirituality.[4]

NOTES

CHAPTER 2: EDUCATION AND THE BIBLE

[1]See E. G. Sihler, *Cicero of Arpinum* (N.Y.: G. E. Stechert, 1933), pp. 267-295. For the status and duties of the proconsul of a province see Edward Gibbon, *The History of the Decline and Fall of the Roman Empire* (N.Y.: Harper & Bros., 1900), 2:284ff.

[2]For the inferences about Apollos as a model of a person educated in both the classics and the Scriptures, I am indebted to my colleague Dr. Walter Jennrich, professor of Greek at Concordia College Wisconsin.

[3]See "Clergy" in *The Oxford English Dictionary*.

[4]Many scholars have developed these points in more detail. See, for example, Herbert N. Schneidau, *Sacred Discontent: The Bible and Western Tradition* (Berkeley: Univ. of California Press, 1977) and Thorleif Boman, *Hebrew Thought Compared to Greek*, trans. Jules C. Moreau (Philadelphia: Westminster Press, 1960).

CHAPTER 3: DANIEL AT THE UNIVERSITY OF BABYLON

[1]A version of this chapter was published in *HIS Magazine*, March 1985, pp. 1-4.

[2]I refer to the notes on the passage in *The New Oxford Annotated Bible* (N.Y.: Oxford Univ. Press, 1973).

[3]I do not intend to rule out civil disobedience in those rare cases when human authorities demand something contrary to the Word of God. In those cases, "We must obey God rather than men" (Acts 5:29).

[4]See also the incident with Arioch in Daniel 2:14, 24, 25.

CHAPTER 4: THE ATTACKS AGAINST CHRISTIANITY
[1]G. K. Chesterton, *Orthodoxy* (Garden City, N.Y.: Doubleday, 1959), p. 84.
[2]*Ibid.*, pp. 85-89.
[3]*Ibid.*, p. 90.
[4]*Ibid.*, p. 15.

CHAPTER 5: THE EXCLUSION OF GOD
[1]Flannery O'Connor, *The Habit of Being: Letters*, ed. Sally Fitzgerald (N.Y.: Farrar, Straus, & Giroux, 1979), p. 149.
[2]Flannery O'Connor, "The Displaced Person," in *The Complete Stories* (N.Y.: Farrar, Straus, & Giroux, 1977), p. 226.
[3]Chesterton, *Orthodoxy*, pp. 25, 26.
[4]Albert Einstein, "The Common Language of Science," in *The Living Language: A Reader*, ed. Linda A. Morris, et al. (N.Y.: Harcourt Brace Jovanovich, 1984), p. 306.
[5]*Ibid.*

CHAPTER 6: TRADITIONALISTS AND PROGRESSIVES
[1]As argued by Schneidau in *Sacred Discontent*.
[2]C. S. Lewis, *Surprised by Joy* (N.Y.: Harcourt, Brace, Jovanovich, 1984), p. 306.
[3]Schneidau, *Sacred Discontent*.
[4]*Ibid.* See Schneidau's introductory chapter, "In Praise of Alienation: The Bible and Western Culture," pp. 1-49.

CHAPTER 7: THE MORAL ISSUES
[1]Chesterton, *Orthodoxy*, p. 107.
[2]Schneidau, *Sacred Discontent*, pp. 15, 16, 116-119.
[3]Chesterton, *Orthodoxy*, p. 107.

CHAPTER 8: INTELLECTUAL COMBAT
[1]For noncreationist critiques of Darwinism see Gordon Rattray Taylor, *The Great Evolution Mystery* (N.Y.: Harper & Row, 1983) and Tom Bethell, "Agnostic Evolutionists: The Taxonomic Case Against Darwin," *Harpers*, February 1985, pp. 49ff.

CHAPTER 9: THE COMMUNION OF THE SAINTS

[1]Peter Berger, "The Class Struggle in American Religion," *Christian Century*, 25 February 1981, p. 198.

[2]*Ibid.*

[3]*Ibid.*

[4]*Ibid.*, p. 199.

[5]For a good discussion of the spiritual dangers of "inner circles," see C. S. Lewis, *Screwtape Letters* (N.Y.: Macmillan, 1958), pp. 53, 54.

[6]I do not intend here to minimize the importance of theological disagreements. I refer not to the "visible Church," which is marred by serious theological schisms, but to the "invisible Church," which is united in Christ.

[7]See C. S. Lewis, "On the Reading of Old Books," in *God in the Dock* (Grand Rapids: Eerdmans, 1970), pp. 200-207.

[8]C. S. Lewis, *Mere Christianity* (N.Y.: Macmillan, 1952), p. 120.

CHAPTER 10: THE MAGICIANS AND THE ENCHANTERS

[1]See Raymon F. Surburg, "The Influence of the Two Delitzsches on Biblical and Near Eastern Studies," *Concordia Theological Quarterly*, 47 (1983): 234-236.

[2]See Michael J. Gorman, *Abortion and the Early Church: Christian, Jewish, and Pagan Attitudes* (Downers Grove, Ill.: InterVarsity Press, 1982).

[3]See my book *The Gift of Art* (Downers Grove, Ill.: InterVarsity Press), 1983, pp. 29-42.

CHAPTER 11: CREATION AND CREATIVITY

[1]Padraic Colum, *Myths of the World* (N.Y.: Grosset & Dunlap, 1959), p. 19.

[2]*Ibid.*, pp. 61-67.

[3]See Chesterton, *Orthodoxy*, pp. 128-134.

[4]I do not intend to minimize the scientific accomplishments of the ancient Greeks, Chinese, and others. Each early scientist, however, had first to demythologize nature and find it trustworthy, a process some, such as Aristotle and Confucius, achieved to a certain extent in other cultures, but which

was accomplished at one stroke where the Bible was accepted. See Schneidau, *Sacred Discontent*, pp. 21-28.

[5]See Gorman, *Abortion and the Early Church*.

[6]See C. S. Lewis, "The Weight of Glory," in *The Weight of Glory and Other Addresses* (Grand Rapids, Mich.: Eerdmans, 1965), p. 15.

[7]See Dorothy L. Sayers, *The Mind of the Maker* (N.Y.: Harcourt, Brace, 1941) and J. R. R. Tolkien, "On Fairy-Stories," in *The Monsters and the Critics and Other Essays*, ed. Christopher Tolkien (Boston: Houghton Mifflin, 1984), pp. 138-157.

[8]For further discussion of what the Bible says about art, see my book *The Gift of Art* (Downers Grove, Ill.: Inter-Varsity Press, 1984).

[9]See Chesterton, *Orthodoxy*, p. 14.

CHAPTER 12: CHRISTIANITY AS AN INTELLECTUAL FRAMEWORK

[1]Chesterton, *Orthodoxy*, p. 92.

[2]*Ibid.*, pp. 96, 97.

[3]Flannery O'Connor, *The Habit of Being*, p. 477. See also the discussion of this letter by Paul Nisly, "Faith Is Not an Electric Blanket," *Christianity Today*, 17 May 1985, p. 22.

[4]Flannery O'Connor, *The Habit of Being*, p. 478.

[5]Blaise Pascal, *Pensees*, fragment 130 [420]. This translation is by Michael Edwards, who discusses the passage in *Towards a Christian Poetics* (Grand Rapids, Mich.: Eerdmans, 1984), pp. 4ff. Edward's book is an excellent example of how the paradoxes of Christianity can be applied in academic scholarship.

[6]Neil Postman, *Teaching as a Conserving Activity* (N.Y.: Delacorte Press, 1979).

[7]Chesterton, *Orthodoxy*, p. 29.

[8]*Ibid.*, pp. 28, 29.

CHAPTER 13: CONCLUSION: LOVING GOD WITH ALL YOUR MIND

[1]C. S. Lewis, "Learning in War-Time," in *The Weight of Glory and Other Addresses*, p. 50.

[2]*Ibid.*

³W. B. Yeats, "The Second Coming," lines 3-8. Quoted from *The Norton Anthology of English Literature*, ed. M. H. Abrams et al. (N.Y.: W. W. Norton, 1979), 2:1973.

⁴For this hope I am indebted to Thomas Russack. See his article, "Is America on the Verge of a New Renaissance?" in *Christian Single Magazine* (Summer 1985).